101 American English Proverbs

Teacher's Manual and
Resource Book

Harry Collis

Illustrations by Mario Risso

National Textbook Company
a division of NTC/CONTEMPORARY PUBLISHING COMPANY
Lincolnwood, Illinois USA

Published by National Textbook Company,
a division of NTC/Contemporary Publishing Company,
4255 West Touhy Avenue,
Lincolnwood (Chicago), Illinois 60646-1975 U.S.A.

Contents

Acknowledgments   vii

Introduction   ix
    The First Step Is Always the Hardest   ix
    Practice Makes Perfect   x
    Necessity Is the Mother of Invention   x

Alphabetical Listing of Proverbs   xii

Section One:
All Together Now   **1**
Birds of a feather flock together * In unity there is strength * It takes two to tango * A man is known by the company he keeps * Misery loves company * There's no place like home * Too many cooks spoil the broth * Two heads are better than one * Two's company, but three's a crowd

Practice Makes Perfect   9
Answer Key   13

Section Two:
Try This   **15**
An apple a day keeps the doctor away * Do as I say, not as I do * If you can't beat them, join them * If you can't stand the heat, get out of the kitchen * Leave well enough alone * Look before you leap * Make hay while the sun shines * Strike while the iron is hot * The way to a man's heart is through his stomach * When in Rome do as the Romans do

Practice Makes Perfect   25
Answer Key   29

Section Three:
Watch Out!   **31**
All that glitters is not gold * Curiosity killed the cat * Don't bite off more than you can chew * Don't bite the hand that feeds you * Don't count your chickens before they're hatched * Don't cry over spilt milk * Don't judge a book by its cover * Don't judge a man until you've walked in his boots * Don't look a gift horse in the mouth * Don't put all your eggs in one basket * Don't put off for tomorrow what you can do today * Don't put the cart before the horse * A miss is as good as a mile * The road to hell is paved with good intentions * Where there's smoke, there's fire

Practice Makes Perfect   45
Answer Key   49

Section Four:

Getting Ahead   **51**

The first step is always the hardest * Forewarned is forearmed * He who hesitates is lost * If at first you don't succeed, try, try again * Necessity is the mother of invention * No pain, no gain * Nothing ventured, nothing gained * The pen is mightier than the sword * Practice makes perfect * Rome wasn't built in a day * The squeaking wheel gets the oil * You're never too old to learn

Practice Makes Perfect   61
Answer Key   65

Section Five:

It Never Works   **67**

Beggars can't be choosers * Clothes do not make the man * A leopard cannot change his spots * Man does not live by bread alone * Money does not grow on trees * One swallow does not a summer make * Too many chiefs, not enough Indians * You can lead a horse to water, but you can't make him drink * You can't have your cake and eat it too * You can't teach an old dog new tricks

Practice Makes Perfect   77
Answer Key   81

Section Six:

It's Human Nature   **83**

The apple doesn't fall far from the tree * Barking dogs seldom bite * Better a live coward than a dead hero * A fool and his money are soon parted * He who laughs last, laughs best * Old habits die hard * One man's gravy is another man's poison * The spirit is willing, but the flesh is weak * There is no honor among thieves * There's more than one way to skin a cat * There's no fool like an old fool * Variety is the spice of life * When the cat's away the mice will play

Practice Makes Perfect   95
Answer Key   99

Section Seven:

Friend or Foe?   **101**

Absence makes the heart grow fonder * Beauty is in the eye of the beholder * Blood is thicker than water * Familiarity breeds contempt * A friend in need is a friend indeed * A friend who shares is a friend who cares * Imitation is the sincerest form of flattery * Love is blind

Practice Makes Perfect   111
Answer Key   115

Section Eight:
Words to Live By   **117**
Actions speak louder than words * Better late than never * Better safe than
sorry * A bird in the hand is worth two in the bush * Charity begins at
home * Haste makes waste * Love makes the world go round * One good
turn deserves another * You have to take the good with the bad * You reap
what you sow

Practice Makes Perfect   127
Answer Key   131

Section Nine:
Some Things Never Change   **133**
After the feast comes the reckoning * Bad news travels fast * The best things
in life are free * The bigger they are, the harder they fall * Good things come
in small packages * The grass is always greener on the other side of the
fence * Hindsight is better than foresight * It never rains but it
pours * Lightning never strikes twice in the same place * Might makes
right * No news is good news * Nothing hurts like the truth * Possession is
nine-tenths of the law * The proof of the pudding is in the eating

Practice Makes Perfect   147
Answer Key   151

Acknowledgments

First of all I would like to thank my wife, Katherine, and my daughter Denise for their feedback and constant support while I was preparing the manuscript for this work.

My appreciation also goes to my colleagues Linda Grondahl, Jose Sevilla, Tom Drain and Alfredo Jordan for acting as catalysts in the writing of several of the scenarios for the manual.

I am particularly grateful to my editor, Kathleen Schultz, for her patience, understanding, and valuable contributions to the realization of this project.

Introduction

The 101 American English Proverbs Learning Cards are designed to promote understanding and spontaneous, appropriate usage of 101 of the most commonly used American English proverbs. Each card contains an illustration that depicts the literal meaning of the proverb in a lively, humorous style. On the back of each card is a dialogue or short passage that uses the proverb in a natural context. These dialogues and passages will help to impart feelings for the usages of the proverbs, while the illustrations will increase the students' retention of the proverbs by highlighting real-life situations in which they are used. In addition, the illustrations will serve as springboards for vocabulary development and spontaneous conversations.

The Learning Cards are numbered and grouped into nine sections based on the general themes of the proverbs. These cards may be used in any order, however, since the contextualizing passages do not progress in difficulty.

This Teacher's Manual and Resource Book contains discussion questions, exercises, and activities, as well as a complete alphabetical listing of all 101 proverbs. Many of the exercises are in the form of blackline masters, which can be removed from this manual and photocopied for classroom use.

The First Step Is Always the Hardest

The material in this manual is divided into nine sections that correspond to the arrangement of the cards in the box. For each proverb, two sets of questions are provided to aid in eliciting and guiding conversation about the elements of the illustration, and to promote a feeling for the proverb by using related imagery. The wording of the questions is natural and often idiomatic in order to expand further the students' vocabulary and to give them a feeling for the colloquial phrasing of questions. The first set of questions, titled *Look before You Leap,* focuses directly on the elements of the proverb as it is depicted in the illustration. The second set of questions, *Make Hay While the Sun Shines,* focuses on expansion of vocabulary and ideas that go beyond the proverb itself, encouraging students to talk "around" the situation presented in the illustration.

Next, in the section titled *A Friend Who Shares...,* the proverb is reinforced in the form of a brief contextualizing passage and a follow-up question. Students may be asked to answer the question individually (orally or in writing) or to discuss their answers in small groups or with the entire class.

Finally, a *Nothing Ventured, Nothing Gained* section is provided for each proverb. These sections contain longer descriptions of situations, which should be read aloud or copied and distributed to the students. The students must then prepare a response to or presentation of the situation, generally in the form of a skit or a written or oral dialogue or monologue. The activities in these sections are well suited for group and pair work.

With imagination on the part of students and teachers, there is ample room for expansion of vocabulary and imagery within the framework of the activities provided for each proverb. Some questions might even be assigned as homework, since they could well require the use of a dictionary or other method of research. It is not necessary to have all students answer all the questions in the *Look before You Leap* or *Make Hay While the Sun Shines* sections. You can select and modify questions as appropriate according to students' abilities or levels of achievement.

Practice Makes Perfect

At the end of each section, a set of review activities, titled *Practice Makes Perfect,* is presented in the form of blackline masters. These activities include multiple-choice, fill-in-the-blank, and matching exercises, as well as word-game activities such as crossword puzzles and word searches. The pages in this section are designed to be removed from the manual, photocopied, and distributed to the students. The activities may be completed in class, with students working individually or in small groups, or assigned for homework. Some teachers may even wish to use them for testing purposes. Answer keys for all the activities are provided at the end of the section.

Necessity Is the Mother of Invention

Below are some suggestions for presenting the proverbs with the Learning Cards. These suggestions are intended only as general guidelines, since working with the cards is certain to inspire many other workable ideas.

1. While holding up a card, ask the students to comment on what they see. They may wish to talk about the individual elements of the picture or about the situation itself. This can be an entirely free discussion, providing ample opportunity for expansion of vocabulary and grammar.
2. Try to lead the students to the thrust of the proverb by highlighting its relationship to the situation portrayed in the illustration.
3. At this point, you might try reading aloud the dialogue or passage printed on the back of the Learning Card, explaining vocabulary and grammar as necessary to ensure comprehension. After hearing the dialogue, the students could experiment with paraphrasing the situation presented in the dialogue.
4. Conclude this part of the discussion by asking the students some or all of the questions from the *Look before You Leap* and *Make Hay While the Sun Shines* sections.
5. Present the material from the *A Friend Who Cares...* section and have the students answer the question orally or in writing.
6. Present the situation described in the *Nothing Ventured, Nothing Gained* section to the students. Working in pairs, groups, or individually, the students can prepare skits or dialogues based on the situation.

After you've covered all the proverbs in a particular section:

7. Select exercises and activities from the *Practice Makes Perfect* section to duplicate and distribute to the students.
8. Play a review game, "Let's Play Round Robin," with the Learning Cards. The purpose of the game is to have all the students in the class contribute to the development of a skit or story based on the proverbs in one section. Divide the class into pairs or teams in such a way that you have an equal number of proverbs per team. Put all the Learning Cards from the section in a bag or box with tall sides. Have one student from

the first team close his or her eyes, draw a card, and show it to the class. This student and the other members of the team must then begin to improvise a dialogue or skit in which the proverb could be used, or make up a story based on the proverb.

On a signal from you, someone from this team must point to the members of another team, indicating that they must immediately take over the development of the dialogue, skit, or story. Again, on a signal from you, the members of the second team must choose a third team to take up the conversation and develop it. The round-robin rotation should continue until each team has contributed its ideas. Then a student from the second team starts the process again by drawing a new card from the bag. The game continues until a story has been developed for each proverb in the bag. A panel of judges (one student from each team) should be selected to "judge" the teams for spontaneity, originality, and imagination—with you providing opinions on the usage of vocabulary and structures. The winning team should receive an appropriate prize such as a night without homework or class time in which to do free reading. This game should both challenge the students and provide them with a sense of accomplishment.

In addition to the Learning Cards and this Teacher's Manual and Resource Book, National Textbook Company publishes the book *101 American English Proverbs*. This book presents the same 101 proverbs found on the Learning Cards. Each proverb appears on a separate page in the book, complete with the same illustration and dialogue or passage presented on the Learning Card. Thus, the book may be used in conjunction with or as an alternative to the Learning Cards. The questions, activities, and exercises provided in this manual are appropriate for use with either the cards or the book.

In addition to the steps for teaching the proverbs outlined above, you might want to incorporate the following activities if the students in your class have the *101 American English Proverbs* book:

1. Read aloud each line of the dialogue or passage, having the students repeat after you in groups, pairs, or individually.

2. Have the students read the proverb and dialogue or passage and study the picture. Then ask them to think of a situation that is similar to the one described in the book.

3. For an effective vocabulary and culture activity, ask the students if they can think of parallel proverbs in their native languages. If they can, have them translate the expressions literally into English and discuss the differences between the various versions of proverbs.

4. Have the students memorize part or all of a dialogue or passage for homework, or have them write a new dialogue or passage based on the proverb.

The focus of the *101 American English Proverbs* book and the *101 American English Proverbs* Learning Cards and Teacher's Manual and Resource Book is basically the development of spontaneous oral expression. It is the hope of the author that the activities contained herein will enable students to improve their oral language skills and to understand and use a wide variety of proverbs, since proverbs reflect many facets of American culture and are an integral part of contemporary American speech.

Alphabetical Listing of Proverbs

A

Absence makes the heart grow fonder (people often feel more affection toward each other when they are apart) 70

Actions speak louder than words (people's actions are more convincing than their words are) 78

After the feast comes the reckoning (people must always pay the price of their excesses) 88

All that glitters is not gold (some things are not as valuable as they appear to be) 20

An apple a day keeps the doctor away (eating an apple every day helps a person to stay healthy) 10

The apple doesn't fall far from the tree (children take after their parents) 57

B

Bad news travels fast (reports of problems and misfortune spread quickly) 89

Barking dogs seldom bite (people who threaten others usually do not hurt them) 58

Beauty is in the eye of the beholder (what seems ordinary or ugly to one person might seem beautiful to another) 71

Beggars can't be choosers (when a person has nothing, he or she must accept whatever help is offered) 47

The best things in life are free (the things that give a person the most happiness don't cost anything) 90

Better a live coward than a dead hero (it's better to run from a life-threatening situation than to fight and risk being killed) 59

Better late than never (it's better to do something late than not to do it at all) 79

Better safe than sorry (it is better to choose a safe course of action than a risky one that could lead to regrets) 80

The bigger they are, the harder they fall (the more important someone is, the more severe are the consequences of his or her failure) 91

A bird in the hand is worth two in the bush (something you already have is better than something you might get) 81

Birds of a feather flock together (people of the same type seem to gather together) 1

Blood is thicker than water (members of the same family share stronger ties with each other than they do with others) 72

C

Charity begins at home (one should take care of one's own family, friends, or fellow citizens before helping other people) 82

Clothes do not make the man (a person should not be judged by the clothes he or she wears) 48

Curiosity killed the cat (it is dangerous to be curious) 21

D

Do as I say, not as I do (follow my advice, but don't follow my example) 11

Don't bite off more than you can chew (don't assume more responsibility than you can handle; don't be overconfident) 22

Don't bite the hand that feeds you (don't hurt someone who takes care of you) 23

Don't count your chickens before they're hatched (don't plan on the successful results of something until those results actually occur) 24

Don't cry over spilt milk (don't grieve about having done something that cannot be undone) 25

Don't judge a book by its cover (don't form an opinion about something based on appearance alone) 26

Don't judge a man until you've walked in his boots (don't criticize a person until you've tried to do the things he does) 27

Don't look a gift horse in the mouth (don't complain about something that is given to you) 28

Don't put all your eggs in one basket (don't risk losing everything at once) 29

Don't put off for tomorrow what you can do today (don't unnecessarily postpone doing something) 30

Don't put the cart before the horse (don't do things in the wrong order) 31

F

Familiarity breeds contempt (when you know people well you will discover their weaknesses and you may come to scorn them) 73

The first step is always the hardest (the most difficult part of accomplishing something is getting started) 35

A fool and his money are soon parted (a foolish person quickly spends his or her money on worthless things) 60

Forewarned is forearmed (being warned about something before it happens allows a person to prepare for it) 36

A friend in need is a friend indeed (a true friend will help you in a time of trouble) 74

A friend who shares is a friend who cares (a true friend unselfishly shares what he or she has) 75

G

Good things come in small packages (small containers can hold objects of great value) 92

The grass is always greener on the other side of the fence (another place or situation always appears to be better than your own) 93

H

Haste makes waste (when one hurries too much, one is likely to do a poor job and have to waste time doing it over) 83

He who hesitates is lost (a person who doesn't act decisively is unlikely to succeed) 37

He who laughs last, laughs best (the person who succeeds in making the last move has the most fun) 61

Hindsight is better than foresight (people see and understand things more clearly after they've happened than before they've happened) 94

I

If at first you don't succeed, try, try again (persevere until you reach your goal) 38

If you can't beat them, join them (if you can't defeat your opponents, join forces with them) 12

If you can't stand the heat, get out of the kitchen (if you can't tolerate the pressures of a particular situation, remove yourself from that situation) 13

Imitation is the sincerest form of flattery (trying to be like someone is the most genuine way of praising that person) 76

In unity there is strength (a group of people with the same goals can accomplish more than individuals can) 2

It never rains but it pours (good and bad things tend to happen in groups) 95

It takes two to tango (when two people work as a team, they are both responsible for the team's successes and failures) 3

L

Leave well enough alone (don't try to improve something that is already satisfactory) 14

A leopard cannot change his spots (a person cannot change his or her basic character once it has been formed) 49

Lightning never strikes twice in the same place (the same misfortune won't happen twice to the same person) 96

Look before you leap (consider all aspects of a situation before you take any action) 15

Love is blind (one sees no faults in the person one loves) 77

Love makes the world go round (when people show respect and consideration for one another, the world is a better place) 84

M

Make hay while the sun shines (take advantage of an opportunity to do something) 16

Man does not live by bread alone (people's psychological needs as well as their physical needs must be satisfied if they are to live) 50

A man is known by the company he keeps (a person is believed to be like the people with whom he or she spends time) 4

Might makes right (the stronger of two opponents will always control the situation) 97

Misery loves company (unhappy people often get satisfaction from having others share their misery) 5

A miss is as good as a mile (losing by a narrow margin is no different than losing by a wide margin) 32

Money does not grow on trees (money is not easily obtained) 51

N

Necessity is the mother of invention (most inventions are created to solve a problem) 39

No news is good news (if one does not hear the outcome of a situation, that outcome must be positive) 98

No pain, no gain (nothing can be accomplished without effort) 40

Nothing hurts like the truth (it is painful to discover an unpleasant truth about oneself) 99

Nothing ventured, nothing gained (you can't achieve anything if you don't try) 41

O

Old habits die hard (it is very difficult to change an established pattern of behavior) 62

One good turn deserves another (a favor should be repaid with another favor) 85

One man's gravy is another man's poison (what is pleasing to one person may not be pleasing to another) 63

One swallow does not a summer make (one piece of evidence is not enough to prove something) 52

P

The pen is mightier than the sword (the written word is more powerful than physical force) 42

Possession is nine-tenths of the law (the person who possesses something has the strongest claim to owning it) 100

Practice makes perfect (doing something many times improves one's skill at it) 43

The proof of the pudding is in the eating (the only way to judge something is to try it) 101

R

The road to hell is paved with good intentions (good intentions don't always lead to good actions) 33

Rome wasn't built in a day (important things do not happen overnight) 44

S

The spirit is willing, but the flesh is weak (a person's body is not always as strong as his or her mind) 64

The squeaking wheel gets the oil (those who complain the loudest get the most attention) 45

Strike while the iron is hot (act at the best possible time) 17

T

There is no honor among thieves (one dishonest person cannot trust another)   65

There's more than one way to skin a cat (there are many ways to achieve a goal)   66

There's no fool like an old fool (a foolish act seems even more foolish when performed by an older person, who should have a lot of wisdom)   67

There's no place like home (a person is happiest with his or her family and friends)   6

Too many chiefs, not enough Indians (too many people are giving orders, and not enough people are following orders)   53

Too many cooks spoil the broth (too many people trying to take care of something can ruin it)   7

Two heads are better than one (two people working together can solve a problem quicker and better than a person working alone)   8

Two's company, but three's a crowd (couples often enjoy their privacy and dislike having a third person around)   9

V

Variety is the spice of life (differences and changes make life enjoyable)   68

W

The way to a man's heart is through his stomach (the way to gain a man's love is by preparing food that he enjoys)   18

When in Rome do as the Romans do (when traveling, follow the customs of the local people)   19

When the cat's away the mice will play (some people will misbehave when they are not being watched)   69

Where there's smoke, there's fire (when there is evidence of a problem, there probably is a problem)   34

Y

You can lead a horse to water, but you can't make him drink (you can propose a course of action to someone, but you can't force that person to accept it)   54

You can't have your cake and eat it too (you can't enjoy the advantages of two conflicting activities at once)   55

You can't teach an old dog new tricks (elderly people can't change their behavior or learn anything new)   56

You have to take the good with the bad (you must accept disappointment along with success)   86

You reap what you sow (the amount of effort you put into something determines how much you will get out of it)   87

You're never too old to learn (a person can learn at any age)   46

Section One

All Together Now

1. Birds of a Feather Flock Together

Look before You Leap

Ask the class the following questions:

What do the two characters in the drawing have in common? What is different about them? Do they both look like types of birds? Does one have the normal features of a bird? What are these features? Can you describe the looks on their faces? How about their sets of "feet"? Which one seems to be friendlier? Why? What is the character on the right holding in his hand? Who or what would you say he is? Do you think they are friends? Why or why not?

Make Hay While the Sun Shines

Ask the class the following questions:

Do you think that the two characters can trust each other? Why or why not? Can you name other types of birds? Do you know anything about the migrating habits of birds? Can you describe a "typical" bird? What do they all have in common? In what ways can one bird distinguish itself from another? Under what circumstances would birds flock together? What kinds of birds are found in tropical climates? What kinds of birds are found in polar regions? What do birds eat? What birds do people often eat? What is the traditional Thanksgiving bird? Which birds frequent oceans, lakes, or ponds? Who or what are the greatest enemies of birds? Why?

A Friend Who Shares...

Present this situation to the students for discussion:

You have just become a member of a group dedicated to the preservation of endangered species of birds. You have always been an animal and nature lover and felt that it was time that you became actively involved in preserving this form of wildlife. What will your friends say about your joining this preservation group?

Nothing Ventured, Nothing Gained

Have the students compose (orally or in writing) a speech or monologue based on the following situation:

This winter a big medical convention is going to be held in your city. The participants plan to discuss the latest advances in the development of a vaccine against a tropical disease of epidemic proportions. What interests do you think the convention participants share? What reasons do they have for attending the convention?

2. In Unity There Is Strength

Look before You Leap

Ask the class the following questions:

Who or what are the three men? What are they wearing? What popular sport are they engaged in? Describe the looks on their faces. What does this indicate about their spirits? Why, do you suppose, are they holding up their arms? Does the fact that their fists are clenched have any significance? Explain.

Make Hay While the Sun Shines

Ask the class the following questions:

Under what circumstances do people clench their fists? Can you name similarities and differences between American football and soccer? What are other popular sports in the United States and in your native country? Can you describe any of the games? What sports are played with a single opponent? What sports are played with one team opposing the other? In your opinion, is it harder or easier to achieve a goal when you are trying to achieve it alone? Explain. Can you describe how people dress for different sports? How could a person's uniform help or hamper him or her when engaging in a particular sport? What's the purpose of a helmet? In what other sports or activities might a helmet be used? When you have accomplished a goal, how do you feel? How do you behave? How would you physically express your satisfaction or emotions?

A Friend Who Shares...

Present this situation to the students for discussion:

Mary has been complaining that her professor is always late for class. She is hesitant to inform the dean about this matter all by herself. She has not yet expressed her concerns to any of her fellow classmates, although she knows that they feel the same as she does. What should Mary realize in this particular situation?

Nothing Ventured, Nothing Gained

Have the students compose (orally or in writing) a speech or monologue based on the following situation:

Phillip has been trying to convince the building superintendent to install air conditioning in the building in which he works, since it becomes so hot in the summer. He has been unable to convince the superintendent by himself and finally decides to solicit the support of his coworkers.

3. It Takes Two to Tango

Look before You Leap

Ask the class the following questions:

What is the couple doing? Describe the position of the man. Does it appear that he will lose his balance? Why? How about the woman? Would you say that she is feeling comfortable? Do you think she is enjoying herself? What makes you think so? What kind of hat is the man wearing? What style is the rest of his outfit? Of what nationality is the outfit typical? Do you see any clues that indicate the man's nationality? What does the woman have between her teeth? Is there a character in a famous opera that she reminds you of? Does it appear that the couple is dancing a modern or a traditional dance? Explain.

Make Hay While the Sun Shines

Ask the class the following questions:

What kind of dance is the couple dancing? Which country did this dance originate in? Can you name and describe other dances that are popular in the United States? In your native country? Do you know of any dances where one dances alone? In couples? As a group? Name some of the elements that go into a dance. What are some of the similarities and differences between folk dances, popular dances, modern dances, and ballet? Do you enjoy dancing? Would you rather dance alone, with a partner, or in a group? Why? Have you ever worked on a project or enterprise with a partner? How did it turn out? Have you ever been blamed for failing to hold up your end of an agreement? Would things have turned out well had you cooperated with the other person?

A Friend Who Shares...

Present this situation to the students for discussion:

Mr. Jones has started a new business but cannot take care of the bookkeeping and the sales end all by himself. He needs his wife's assistance to successfully run the business. What might he suggest to her?

Nothing Ventured, Nothing Gained

Have the students compose (orally or in writing) a speech or monologue based on the following situation:

Jack had become mixed up with some of the local hoodlums. His mother blamed his father for not setting a better example for Jack to follow. However, Jack's mother was never at home to look after the needs of her son and to keep tabs on his outside activities away from school. Jack's father felt that he should not take the entire blame for his son's waywardness.

4.   A Man Is Known by the Company He Keeps

Look before You Leap

Ask the class the following questions:

Who are the two adult characters in the illustration? Can you describe them? Who is the little girl focusing her attention on? Why? Why would the girl not want to be associated with the other character? How does he react to the fact that the little girl is ignoring him?

Make Hay While the Sun Shines

Ask the class the following questions:

Can you name some positive, desirable traits in a person? What are some negative traits? Have you ever been judged because of your association with certain groups or types of people? What were the circumstances? Can you name some reasons why someone would associate with a particular person or group? Do you think that because someone does spend his or her time with certain friends or groups of people that he or she is necessarily like them? Explain. Is it fair to form an opinion about people based on how they are dressed or what they look like? Would your judgment be more accurate if you based it on behavior, rather than appearance? Do you think that there is room for error on your part? What would you do or say to someone if you realized that you had misjudged them.

A Friend Who Shares...

Present this situation to the students for discussion:

Kevin started keeping company with a group of kids who were always cutting classes at school, yet he, himself, was a good, conscientious student. What might his parents tell him?

Nothing Ventured, Nothing Gained

Have the students compose (orally or in writing) a speech or monologue based on the following situation:

Mr. Smith has been a Boy Scout leader and has been involved in many community activities. He is admired for his contributions and leadership qualities. He has decided to run for mayor of the city and has appointed you as one of his campaign managers. Discuss his chances for being elected to the position.

5.   Misery Loves Company

Look before You Leap

Ask the class the following questions:

What is one of the men hanging from? What does he have around his wrists? Can you describe his appearance? Why do you think he is there? How do you suppose he is feeling? What is happening to the man in the middle? Why do you think that he is being led to this place? Can you describe his feelings? Does it seem that he has done something wrong? What could he have done? Who is the man accompanying him? How is he dressed? What is he holding? What could it be used for? Do you think that the man on the wall will feel better, knowing that he will be joined by someone else? Explain why or why not.

Make Hay While the Sun Shines

Ask the class the following questions:

Can you name some things that make a person miserable? How about things that make people happy? What kinds of people go to prison? Have you ever felt miserable? Under what circumstances? Has anyone ever tried to comfort you? Explain. Have you ever been in a negative situation and felt better knowing that someone else is in the same position? Talk about your reactions. If you feel happy about something would you want others to share in your happiness? Why? How do you react to someone who is feeling badly? If you were in their same predicament, do you think they would feel better knowing that you were miserable, too?

A Friend Who Shares...

Present this situation to the students for discussion:

Susanne has just found out that she was not accepted at the university of her choice. John, her friend, has been sulking all week because he didn't get a promotion at work. John calls Susanne and wants to talk to her over lunch. What would prompt him to do this?

Nothing Ventured, Nothing Gained

Have the students compose (orally or in writing) a speech or monologue based on the following situation:

Recently Mr. Templeton had been discharged from his position as company treasurer for mismanaging the company's funds. It has come to his attention that his good friend, Luke, had lost his job as athletic director of a health club. Mr. Templeton decides to call on his friend and discuss their situations, and to explore possibilities for other employment.

6. There's No Place like Home

Look before You Leap

Ask the class the following questions:

What is the animal in the drawing? How do you think it is feeling? Why? Does it appear that it has any of the conveniences of a modern home? What kind of a "roof" is on its home? What is on the "roof"? Is its home a permanent one? Explain. Do you think its home requires periodic care to stay in shape? Why or why not?

Make Hay While the Sun Shines

Ask the class the following questions:

Can you describe different kinds of dwellings? What type of maintenance do they require? What are some of the costs involved in maintaining a home? What are some articles of furniture that are found in almost every home? What, do you think, are the basic necessities? What articles of furniture do you consider "luxury items"? What are their purposes? Can you name some appliances that make life more comfortable? In which ways do they facilitate daily living? Have you ever been away from home? How have you felt? In addition to furniture and appliances, what other factors make your home a place where you like to be? What does a home represent to you? Do you think it would be difficult to relocate? Why or why not? Under what circumstances might it be advantageous to live away from your original home?

A Friend Who Shares...

Present this situation to the students for discussion:

Estelle was brought up in a small town in the midwestern United States. She has been studying in Paris, France, for a year but misses all of her friends and has gotten terribly homesick. What is she probably thinking?

Nothing Ventured, Nothing Gained

Have the students compose (orally or in writing) a speech or monologue based on the following situation:

Mr. and Mrs. Carlotsis had migrated to the United States thirty years ago. Both of their children were born in the new land. After much hard work and sacrifice, Mr. Carlotsis was able to develop a very successful delicatessen business. Although he lived comfortably and happily with his family, he had never ceased to long for the land of his birth. Now that his children were grown and married, he decided to retire and go back to spend the rest of his years in his native land.

7.   Too Many Cooks Spoil the Broth

Look before You Leap

Ask the class the following questions:

Who are the people in the illustration? What are they wearing? Where are they? What are the two women holding, and what are they doing? What is the man holding, and what is he doing? Can you tell what they are making? Do they appear satisfied with their efforts? Explain why or why not. Does it seem that what they are preparing will turn out satisfactorily?

Make Hay While the Sun Shines

Ask the class the following questions:

Do you like to cook? Are you a good cook? Where did you learn? Can you cook ethnic dishes? Which dishes do you prefer? American or ethnic? Why? Do you prefer home-cooked meals or fast-food meals? Why? On what occasions would you prefer fast-food meals over home-cooked meals? On what occasions would you prefer home-cooked meals? Can you name the ingredients in one of your favorite dishes? Can you describe how it is prepared? What are names of some utensils used to prepare food? How are the utensils used? When you are preparing a meal, do you like to do it alone or do you welcome someone else's help? Explain. Do you think that people mean well when they offer their help? Are there occasions when someone else's help would be welcome? Explain. On what occasions would you resent a helping hand, even if well intentioned?

A Friend Who Shares...

Present this situation to the students for discussion:

Mr. Rodriguez has spent a good deal of the morning organizing the tools and accessories in his workshop. Mrs. Rodriguez, wanting to help him, misplaces many of his tools. What could Mr. Rodriguez say to her to allow him to finish the job alone?

Nothing Ventured, Nothing Gained

Have the students compose (orally or in writing) a speech or monologue based on the following situation:

Virginia is a piano teacher and files her sheet music by composer and by degree of difficulty. She is in the process of updating her files when a couple of friends who know nothing about music drop by and offer to give her a hand. Although they are good friends, and well meaning, Virginia would be much better off without their help.

8.   Two Heads are Better Than One

Look before You Leap

Ask the class the following questions:

Can you describe the expression on the man's face? Would you say that he looks distressed? What is he holding in his arm? Do you see any similarities between the two heads? Describe them. Does it seem to you that something bad had happened to the man? Can you justify your opinion? Can you think of any reasons why the man would want to have an additional head?

Make Hay While the Sun Shines   Ask the class the following questions:

The head is a part of the body; can you name other parts of the head? What are their functions? What are some of the functions of the brain? Do you think that a person would be smarter if it were possible for him or her to have two brains? Why? Have you ever been stuck on a problem? Describe the circumstances. Were you able to solve it alone, or did you solicit aid from another person? Did that person help or impede your efforts? Describe what happened. Have you ever been asked to give advice in helping someone make a decision? Describe the situation. How were you able to help this person? Did he or she profit by your input?

A Friend Who Shares . . .   Present this situation to the students for discussion:

You are a travel agent and have been trying to plan the itinerary of a client. Unfortunately, you've had trouble booking accommodations in certain out-of-the-way destinations. You want to solicit the expertise of your partner. How would you approach her?

Nothing Ventured, Nothing Gained   Have the students compose (orally or in writing) a speech or monologue based on the following situation:

Imagine that you are a designer for a new shopping center. The height of some of the buildings, and the location of some of the stores has been in question. Thus far, you have been unable to decide on an appropriate course of action, and you call in one of the architects and a member of the planning committee to help you make some decisions. Discuss the proceedings.

9.   Two's Company, but Three's a Crowd

Look before You Leap   Ask the class the following questions:

Who is the man walking into the room? What is he doing? How do you think he feels about seeing his friends? Can you describe the couple sitting on the chair? Would you say that they want company? Why or why not? Can you describe the expressions on the faces of the man and woman? How do you think they feel? Does it appear that the couple expected the interruption? Explain.

Make Hay While the Sun Shines   Ask the class the following questions:

Have you ever interrupted a conversation? Under what circumstances? What were the reactions of those engaged in conversation? Do you think it is okay to drop in on someone unannounced? Explain. Can you think of any occasions where an interruption or an unexpected visit might be embarrassing? Are there ever any occasions where an unexpected visit might be welcome? Have you ever felt that you wanted to be alone with another person? Under what circumstances? What would you feel toward someone who intruded on your privacy? Do you think that it is easy or difficult to resume a private discussion after being interrupted? Explain.

A Friend Who Shares...   Present this situation to the students for discussion:

Frank and Elsa had been deep in conversation about their plans for their honeymoon, when a group of well-wishing friends unexpectedly barged in for drinks and small talk. What would Frank and Elsa think about this unannounced intrusion on their conversation?

Nothing Ventured, Nothing Gained   Have the students compose (orally or in writing) a speech or monologue based on the following situation:

Mr. Mayfair has been concerned about his son's plans for college and has decided to talk to him about the advantages and disadvantages of living in a dorm versus renting an apartment and sharing the expenses with a roommate. In the middle of their conversation his son's friend walks in and asks for help with his math homework.

Practice Makes Perfect

I. Select the best proverb to complete each sentence. In some cases, more than one answer is possible.

1. —Do you mind if my sister comes to the movie with us tonight?

    —I'd rather go with just you. You know, _____ .
    a. too many cooks spoil the broth
    b. two heads are better than one
    c. two's company, but three's a crowd

2. —You shouldn't spend so much time with that wild group of kids. Don't forget,

    _____ .
    a. in unity there is strength
    b. A man is known by the company he keeps
    c. two heads are better than one

3. Jamie and her friends are all good athletes. I guess it's true that _____ .
    a. birds of a feather flock together
    b. misery loves company
    c. there's no place like home

4. Will you please look at this tax form with me? Maybe we can figure it out together, since

    _____ .
    a. in unity there is strength
    b. two heads are better than one
    c. there's no place like home

5. Paul likes to travel a lot, but Christa thinks _____ .
    a. it takes two to tango
    b. misery loves company
    c. there's no place like home

6. —Do you need any help?

    —No, thank you. _____ . I can finish this by myself.
    a. Too many cooks spoil the broth
    b. Misery loves company
    c. Two's company, but three's a crowd

7. If we all stick together, I'm sure Mrs. Perkins will believe our story. After all,

    _____ .
    a. birds of a feather flock together
    b. it takes two to tango
    c. in unity there is strength

8. Rafael was upset because he failed the English test. Since _____ , he felt a little better when he heard that Angelique failed it, too.
   a. misery loves company
   b. a man is known by the company he keeps
   c. it takes two to tango

9. Marie complained to Claude that their dinner was cold. "It's not all my fault," he said.

   "_____ . You didn't come home from work on time."
   a. Birds of a feather flock together
   b. It takes two to tango
   c. A man is known by the company he keeps

II. Match the situation in column A with the proverb in column B.

A	B
1. Where should we go for our vacation?	a. Kind of strange. I guess too many cooks spoil the broth.
2. Alicia is helping Yolanda with her homework.	b. That's a good idea. Two heads are better than one.
3. Yesterday Mark was really upset about breaking up with Tiffany, but today he seems happier.	c. I'm not surprised. Birds of a feather flock together.
4. At our school, the good students all eat lunch at the same table.	d. She's your daughter, too. It takes two to tango.
5. The students went to the principal's office together to explain what happened.	e. Why not stay here? There's no place like home.
6. Don't blame me if you don't like the way Martha behaves.	f. Not really. Miranda sat and talked to us the whole time. She must now know that two's company, but three's a crowd.
7. Tanya doesn't get very high grades, but everyone thinks she's a good student.	g. That's because her friends are all honor students. A man is known by the company he keeps.
8. Denise and Gary helped me make this casserole. How does it taste?	h. That's because misery loves company. He found out that Tim and Michelle broke up, too.
9. Did you and Yohei have a good time at the party last night?	i. None of them wanted to go alone, but they believed that in unity there is strength.

III. Find and circle the italicized parts of these proverbs. Be sure to look horizontally, vertically, and diagonally.

birds of a feather flock *together*
in unity there is strength
it takes two to tango
a man is known by the company he keeps
misery loves company
there's *no place like home*
too many cooks spoil the broth
two heads are better than one
two's company, but *three's a crowd*

```
b x f j o o r t s g q u a i p u z c i m g d y
i t t y a m a n i s k n o w n l m b c e w a n
h e w r q w k l p i x s g s o u y z x c v b a
a s d o g h j l o p y e n e p r s u t s d g p
f i b v h i p l u e s r a o l r n o i l o z m
y u n i v e w e l s n a t p a b a w s v c m o
t h r e e s a c r o w d o m c o p d e e t s c
w m a y e w o d v k o w t n e y o e i s r l s
o p o q w o i e s r u y o t l h i f e e l o e
s k o o c y n a m o o t w z i x c e h f s g v
c p a o s i e j f l v c t m k e h t n b e a o
o a i f l g h o i v e n s w e c e o t x i t l
m b e i n g p e w q u r e s h g s t e r p w y
p t r i m n i p w e f g k t o i l k n s v e r
a r e w e r q p o k l s a t m j i o s l c f e
n b i r d s o f a f e a t h e r m n b v c x s
y z a z w o i e r s a f t i m o n e t s b p i
i n u n i t y t h e r e i s s t r e n g t h m
```

Answer Key

I. 1. c.   6. a.   II. 1. e.   6. d.
  2. b.   7. c.   2. b.   7. g.
  3. a.   8. a.   3. h.   8. a.
  4. b.   9. b.   4. c.   9. f.
  5. c.   5. i.

```
b x f j o o r t s g q u a i p u z c i m g d y
i t t y a m a n i s k n o w n l m b c e w a n
h e w r q w k l p i x s g s o u y z x c v b a
a s d o g h j l o p y e n e p r s u t s d g p
f i b v h i p l u e s r a o l r n o i l o z m
y u n i v e w e l s n a t p a b a w s v c m o
t h r e e s a c r o w d o m c o p d e e t s c
w m a y e w o d v k o w t n e y o e i s r l s
o p o q w o i e s r u y o t l h i f e e l o e
s k o o c y n a m o o t w z i x c e h f s g v
c p a o s i e j f l v c t m k e h t n b e a o
o a i f l g h o i v e n s w e c e o t x i t l
m b e i n g p e w q u r e s h g s t e r p w y
p t r i m n i p w e f g k t o i l k n s v e r
a r e w e r q p o k l s a t m j i o s l c f e
n b i r d s o f a f e a t h e r m n b v c x s
y z a z w o i e r s a f t i m o n e t s b p i
i n u n i t y t h e r e i s s t r e n g t h m
```

Section Two
Try This

10.   An Apple a Day Keeps the Doctor Away

Look before You Leap

Ask the class the following questions:

What is the boy eating? Does he seem to be enjoying it? What building is he walking past? Who is standing in the window? Does it appear that the boy is going to enter the building? Explain why or why not. Does it seem to you that the person in the window was expecting the boy? Explain your opinion. Judging from the boy's appearance, what would you say is the state of his health? Can you justify your answer?

Make Hay While the Sun Shines

Ask the class the following questions:

In addition to the apple, what other fruits can you name? What are the benefits of eating fruit? Doctors say that fruit is a necessary part of your daily diet. What other foods are essential for good health? Besides eating properly, in what other ways can a person maintain his or her health? Have you ever felt tired or had a low energy level? What do you think was the cause? What did you do to start feeling better? Do you think it is important to get eight hours of sleep every night? Why or why not? Do you think everyone needs eight hours of sleep every night? Can some people do with less? What have you personally observed? Do you believe that by eating apples you won't ever have to go see a doctor? Explain.

A Friend Who Shares . . .

Present this situation to the students for discussion:

Lately, Daniel has been sleepy and inattentive in class. He complains of headaches and general malaise. His teacher takes note of these symptoms and thinks that perhaps Daniel should improve his diet. What recommendation does he lightheartedly make to Daniel?

Nothing Ventured, Nothing Gained

Have the students compose (orally or in writing) a speech or monologue based on the following situation:

Stephanie has had mild illnesses off and on for over six months. She has seen her doctor several times, but she hasn't been able to find anything wrong. One of her friends suggests that Stephanie try changing her diet to include at least three fruits a day, including at least one apple.

11.   Do As I Say, Not As I Do

Look before You Leap

Ask the class the following questions:

What is the woman doing? Judging from the expression in her eyes, how would you say she is feeling? Why do you suppose she has her hands on her hips? How about the girl? What is she about to do? How can you tell? What does the expression in the girl's eyes reveal about what she is preparing to do? Does it seem that the girl was being open about what she was preparing to do? If not, why not? Does it seem to you that the girl is acting independently? Explain. Do you think the woman is pleased by what she sees? Explain why or why not.

Make Hay While the Sun Shines

Ask the class the following questions:

Do you smoke? Why or why not? Why do you suppose that people do smoke? Can you think of any reasons that smokers would have to justify their habit of smoking? In your native country do many people smoke? At what age do they usually start? Do more men than women smoke? Do you know the ratio? Why do you think that people start to smoke? How about people who don't smoke? Do you think that they are bothered by people who do? In what way? Would you say that nonsmokers are healthier than smokers? State your reasons for your opinion. Do you think that you personally are an independent thinker, or do you expect people to advise you before you decide to take a course of action? While growing up, do you believe that you have had good role models to follow? What qualities or traits in them did you admire? Did you want to be like them? Have you ever been disappointed in a person whom you looked up to? Describe. How did you react? Would you still follow the advice of someone doing something wrong, even though you admired them greatly for other things? Why or why not?

A Friend Who Shares...

Present this situation to the students for discussion:

Janet had a bad habit of arriving late for appointments. One day when one of her friends arrived late for an appointment with her, Janet chided her for being so late. Her friend promptly responded that she was just following Janet's example. What would be Janet's retort?

Nothing Ventured, Nothing Gained

Have the students compose (orally or in writing) a speech or monologue based on the following situation:

Although he was a good father, Mr. Muldavy had a small drinking problem. No matter how hard he tried, he was not always successful in concealing his drinking from his family. One day when Mr. Muldavy arrived home unexpectedly he caught his teenage son drinking an alcoholic beverage in the kitchen. Mr. Muldavy was terribly upset and began to reprimand his son for doing something that would be so harmful to his health.

12. If You Can't Beat Them, Join Them

Look before You Leap

Ask the class the following questions:

What are the two men doing? How is each one dressed? Judging from their expressions, how would you say they are feeling toward each other? What do they have in common? Which one of the two would you say is the most successful? Why do you think so? Can you describe the vehicle of each one? According to the illustration, which one of the two do you think is going to help the other? How do you think he could do this? In what way will the person being helped benefit from the other's generosity?

Make Hay While the Sun Shines

Ask the class the following questions:

Do you like ice cream? If so, what do you like about it? If not, what don't you like about it? Can you describe how it tastes? What ingredients is ice cream made of? Can you name other dairy foods? Can you name different ways in which ice cream is served? Have you ever been in competition with someone else? Over what? What was the outcome? Do you think it's worth the time and effort to overcome an opponent or a competitor? Why or why not? If you don't get your way, what do you do? Have you ever admired an opponent for doing what you cannot do? What prompted your admiration? Do you think it is better to give in rather than continue a losing battle? Explain both sides of the question.

A Friend Who Shares...

Present this situation to the students for discussion:

Steven has recently graduated with a degree in architecture but seems to be having trouble drumming up clients. Most of the business has been going to the two established architectural firms of the city. What would one of his friends suggest that he do if he wants to continue working in his profession?

Nothing Ventured, Nothing Gained

Have the students compose (orally or in writing) a speech or monologue based on the following situation:

Mr. Muller, a renowned pianist, came to live in Huntsville and planned to earn his living by establishing a piano studio and doing limited concertizing. However, much to his dismay, he found that he was competing for students with the local conservatory of music and that his plans were not working out. One day he decided to visit the conservatory and inquire about a position as one of the staff pianists.

13. If You Can't Stand the Heat, Get Out of the Kitchen

Look before You Leap

Ask the class the following questions:

How is the woman dressed? What do you think she was doing? Where? What do you suppose happened to make her run? What might be the temperature in the house? What makes you think so? Does it appear to you that she was successfully completing her project? Can you explain what might have happened?

Make Hay While the Sun Shines

Ask the class the following questions:

When you see smoke what do you think is happening? Have you ever tried to run away from anything? Describe the circumstances. How did you feel? Can you give reasons why someone might try to run away from something? Have you ever been in a pressing situation? What was it? How did you handle it? Did you stay with it and try to control it or did you simply leave it? If you were to complain about something and you could not change what was happening, what would you do? Why? Do you think that it is better to stick with a difficult occupation because it pays a lot of money, or do you think it would be better to look for a job with less pressure and less money? Explain your position and reasons for your selection.

A Friend Who Shares...

Present this situation to the students for discussion:

If a friend of yours were constantly complaining to you that he had too much homework in a certain course in school, what advice would you give him?

Nothing Ventured, Nothing Gained

Have the students compose (orally or in writing) a speech or monologue based on the following situation:

Dorothy had always been attracted by the lights and glitter of the big city, so she moved into a condo that was located near the nightclubs and theaters. At first she was enchanted with the parties, loud music, and plays; however, she soon developed a strong aversion to the constant noise and hustle and bustle of her neighborhood. She longed for the peace and quiet of the suburbs and moved to a small town right outside the city.

14.   Leave Well Enough Alone

Look before You Leap

Ask the class the following questions:

What is the lady trying to do? Does it appear that she will succeed? In what position is her tongue? What does this indicate? What is on the table? How are they stacked? Can you describe this "structure"? Does it seem sturdy? What do you think will happen if she tries to place that last card on top of the others? Why do you think she is trying to place that last card instead of being satisfied with the "structure" as it is?

Make Hay While the Sun Shines

Ask the class the following questions:

What card games do you know? Can you describe any of them? Why do you think that people play cards? Are card games popular in your native country? Can you name the four suits in cards? Are card games played exclusively for enjoyment and entertainment or for other purposes as well? What might they be? Are you always satisfied with what you accomplish? If not, what do you do? Are you generally successful in your efforts? Explain. Why do you think that anyone would even attempt to improve something that was already acceptable? Have you ever tried to make something "better" that was already in a satisfactory condition? Explain.

A Friend Who Shares...

Present this situation to the students for discussion:

Mr. Harding has zealously taken care of every detail for the reception honoring the ambassador of Proverbiania, yet he doesn't seem totally satisfied with the arrangements he has made and keeps on trying to do more. What might his employees tell him to do?

Nothing Ventured, Nothing Gained

Have the students compose (orally or in writing) a speech or monologue based on the following situation:

Mr. and Mrs. Featherstone employed the services of an interior decorator to furnish the living room and dining room of their new home. The rooms were done to perfection; nevertheless, Mrs. Featherstone keeps trying to make changes here and there. These "changes" really mar the overall decor of the rooms. Mr. Featherstone finally steps in and tells his wife to stop rearranging the room.

15.   Look before You Leap

Look before You Leap

Ask the class the following questions:

Who is the girl? What is she doing? Into what is she diving? What do you suppose the weather is like? Where did she dive from? Do you think she looked before jumping? Had she looked, what would she have seen? What do you think will happen to the girl? Do you believe that the girl thought it would be safe to take a dive into the pool?

Make Hay While the Sun Shines

Ask the class the following questions:

Do you know how to swim? Where did you learn? Where can one go swimming? Where do you prefer to swim? Why? Where do you think it is the safest to go swimming? Why? And where is it the most dangerous to go swimming? Why? Do you know when a person should *not* go swimming? Have you ever done something foolish? Can you describe the situation? What made you do it? How did you feel afterward? Did you consider all aspects of the situation before taking any action? Do you think that most people really think about what they do before they do it? Why? Why not? Why do you think that a person might not look thoroughly into a contemplated course of action? Would it be because of laziness? Lack of foresight? What do you think?

A Friend Who Shares...   Present this situation to the students for discussion:

The Garcias saw a wonderful home that they thought might be right for them just outside the city, but it was near the airport and the freeway entrance. Before buying they went to talk to some of the people living in the area. What do you think they told the Garcias because of the noise from the airplanes and the traffic on the streets where children usually like to play?

Nothing Ventured, Nothing Gained   Have the students compose (orally or in writing) a speech or monologue based on the following situation:

Paul was all set to buy a new car when he visited a used-car lot and saw a beautifully polished almost-brand-new looking model of the same car he was thinking of getting. He was on the point of buying it since the price was much less than that of a new car, but first he decided to consult with a mechanic friend of his about the wisdom of such an action. What do you think his friend told him?

16.   Make Hay While the Sun Shines

Look before You Leap   Ask the class the following questions:

Who or what is on the pole? What is he made of? Where is he? Why is he there? What kind of expression does he have on his face? What kind of plants do you think are growing around the pole? What is the weather like? How can you tell? How would you react if you saw a figure on a stick? Would you be frightened? Why or why not?

Make Hay While the Sun Shines   Ask the class the following questions:

What kind of crops do farmers plant in their fields? Can you name any? Do you know how they take care of their crops? What do they do to raise them? How do they protect them? Do you know of any reasons why crops might fail? Excluding natural causes, what animals or insects can harm crops? How? In what type of weather do crops thrive? Why? What type of weather can destroy crops? Why? What things frighten you? What do you do when you are frightened? Have you ever put off doing something? Why? Do you believe that opportunity knocks only once? Explain. Have you ever failed to take advantage of an opportunity that unexpectedly came your way? Discuss. Would you have profited or have been better off by taking advantage of this opportunity? Can you discuss how you perhaps lost out by not availing yourself of an occasion to get involved in a particular activity or project?

A Friend Who Shares...   Present this situation to the students for discussion:

Mr. Jennison wants to buy school clothes for the kids. Her friend Shirley has just found out that one of the department stores is having a half-off sale tomorrow from 10 to 12. When Shirley sees Mrs. Jennison later on what do you think she will advise her to do?

Nothing Ventured, Nothing Gained

Have the students compose (orally or in writing) a speech or monologue based on the following situation:

Camille is a star pupil in French. Her teacher is taking a number of the students on a tour of Paris and other major cities of France this summer and invites Camille to come along. Most of the students' expenses are to be paid by private doners and by proceeds from the French club. Camille hesitates to join the group because of a previous commitment for the summer. Her teacher points out what a rewarding experience it would be and asks Camille to reconsider her decision.

17.   Strike While the Iron Is Hot

Look before You Leap

Ask the class the following questions:

What is the man in the illustration? How is he dressed? Describe the articles of clothing on his head, legs, and feet. What does he have in his hands? Is it hot or cold? How can you tell? What is it used for? What is he chasing? How can you tell? Why do you think the animal is running away? Do you think the man wants to hurt the animal? Why is he chasing it? Explain.

Make Hay While the Sun Shines

Ask the class the following questions:

Do you know what a cowboy is? In what regions of the United States are they found? Do you have any idea of how they live? How do they occupy themselves? Do you think that cowboys are now as numerous as they were in previous years? Explain why or why not. In which other country can cowboys be found? What are they called? Where do they live? Why are cattle and horses branded? Can you name other livestock? What do livestock usually eat? Where do they graze? What other animals can be found on a farm or ranch? Have you ever taken advantage of an opportunity to accomplish something? What were the circumstances? In your opinion when is the most effective time to initiate a course of action if you want it to turn out favorably? Why? Do you think that an opportunity missed is an opportunity lost? Explain.

A Friend Who Shares . . .

Present this situation to the students for discussion:

Air fares to Europe have never been lower. The Metcalfes are planning a trip to Italy and Greece and are waiting to buy their tickets right before the date of their departure. What would you advise them to do, given the present situation?

Nothing Ventured, Nothing Gained

Have the students compose (orally or in writing) a speech or monologue based on the following situation:

The owners of Super Stereo have just lost their lease and must move to another location. Because of this, they must liquidate as much of their stock in stereo equipment as possible. You have been holding off on buying a compact disc player and have just heard about the liquidation sale.

18.   The Way to a Man's Heart Is Through His Stomach

Look before You Leap

Ask the class the following questions:

What is the man preparing to do? How do you know? From his appearance would you say he is enthusiastic about what he is preparing to do? How can you tell? Who is the woman? What has she placed on the table? Does it appear that she is planning on sitting down at the table with the man? Explain. What is she wearing? What has she prepared? Would you say that she is looking forward to serving what she has prepared? What do you suppose is under the cover of the platter? How do you think it will taste?

Make Hay While the Sun Shines

Ask the class the following questions:

What implements is the man holding? Can you name other implements used for eating? What do you place on the table when setting it for guests? Can you name any kitchen utensils that are used for the preparation of food? How are they used? Can you name some of your favorite dishes? What ingredients are used in preparing them? In your family is food prepared to please any one particular member of the family? If so, why? What effect do you think that a good meal would have on a person's frame of mind? Why? What do you think would attract a man to a woman more: her cooking or her looks? Why? Can you name other characteristics or personality traits that might attract one person to another? Do you think that you would be loved more if you happened to be a gourmet cook? Why or why not?

A Friend Who Shares...

Present this situation to the students for discussion:

Guillermo has been upset with his wife for overspending at the department stores. She wants to restablish their compatible relationship and get on his good side again, so she decides to visit the supermarket. What do you suppose she is planning to do and why?

Nothing Ventured, Nothing Gained

Have the students compose (orally or in writing) a dialogue based on the following situation:

Cheryl knows that Tom is on the verge of proposing marriage to her. They have been going around for almost a year and although Tom has seen all sides of her personality, he has yet to taste her cooking. Cheryl is anxious to have Tom take that "final step" to ask for her hand in marriage and has gone all out to prepare a gourmet dinner—with vintage wine and all.

19.   When in Rome Do As the Romans Do

Look before You Leap

Ask the class the following questions:

What are the two men doing? Are they dressed the same? Can you describe what each one is wearing? What does their manner of dress tell you about the two men? Does the man on the left seem to be enjoying himself? Why do you think he is behaving in that manner? Does it seem to you that this is something that he would ordinarily do? Explain. Do you think that the man on the right is behaving in a strange way, or do you think that he feels comfortable doing what he is doing? Explain.

Make Hay While the Sun Shines

Ask the class the following questions:

Have you ever done something that seemed strange or even ridiculous to some-one else? If so, describe when and under what circumstances. If not, why not? Do you personally feel comfortable or uncomfortable when you are with a group of people or in someone else's home? Describe why you might feel either one way or the other. Do you think that knowing a foreign language is an as-set? Explain why. Have you ever behaved in a way that is not natural for you just to be accepted by a certain individual or by a group of individuals? Ex-plain under what circumstances. Do you think that a person can modify his behavior? When? On what occasions? Have you ever traveled abroad? If so, describe what you thought of each country you visited. Did you have any diffi-culties adjusting to an unfamiliar environment? How did you react to differ-ences in dress, speech, cuisine, or mannerisms? Did you find it easy or difficult to accept ways different from your own? What were the most difficult things to accept? What were the easiest? What adjustments did you personally have to make when you came to this country?

A Friend Who Shares...

Present this situation to the students for discussion:

Mr. and Mrs. Davis are not very experienced travelers and are planning a trip to several exotic countries. You, as their friend, want to make sure that they enjoy their trip and that they not expect things to be as they are at home. What would you advise them to do?

Nothing Ventured, Nothing Gained

Have the students compose (orally or in writing) a dialogue based on the fol-lowing situation:

Alfredo and Chiqui are experienced travelers. When they first started traveling they had experienced difficulties adjusting to the local customs of the coun-tries they were visiting and had even gotten sick by sampling the local cuisine. Nevertheless, their passion for seeing the world drove them to continue travel-ing to far off, exotic lands. To feel more comfortable in a culture other than their own, they picked up a conversational knowledge of several languages; but most important of all—they learned to accept and not criticize ways that were on many occasions so different from their own.

Name_____ Date_____

Practice Makes Perfect

I. Select the best proverb to complete each sentence. In some cases, more than one answer is possible.

1. You shouldn't eat so much junk food. I know I eat a lot of candy, but please _____ .
   a. do as I say, not as I do
   b. strike while the iron is hot
   c. make hay while the sun shines

2. —Why are you baking a cake?

   —It's for Manuel. I want to impress him, and _____ .
   a. when in Rome do as the Romans do
   b. if you can't beat them, join them
   c. the way to a man's heart is through his stomach

3. Quit messing with your hair. It looks fine. Just _____ .
   a. look before you leap
   b. leave well enough alone
   c. make hay while the sun shines

4. —Jared is never sick.

   —That's because he has a healthy diet _____ .
   a. An apple a day keeps the doctor away
   b. If you can't stand the heat, get out of the kitchen
   c. When in Rome do as the Romans do

5. —Why are you wearing that crazy outfit?

   —This is how everyone dresses around here. _____ .
   a. Do as I say, not as I do
   b. Make hay while the sun shines
   c. When in Rome do as the Romans do

6. —Why are you going to the mall? You hate shopping!

   —I know, but it's the only thing my friends want to do. So I decided _____ .
   a. if you can't stand the heat, get out of the kitchen
   b. look before you leap
   c. if you can't beat them, join them

7. —It's a great day to wash the car.

   —You're right. Let's _____ .
   a. make hay while the sun shines
   b. leave well enough alone
   c. look before you leap

8. —I hate my job. I'm always so tired when I get home.

   —Why don't you quit? _____ .
   a. When in Rome do as the Romans do
   b. If you can't stand the heat, get out of the kitchen
   c. The way to a man's heart is through his stomach

9. Before you buy a used car, have a mechanic check it for you. _____ !
   a. Make hay while the sun shines
   b. Leave well enough alone
   c. Look before you leap

10. Mom's in a good mood today, so I'm going to ask her to buy me that new sweater. I want to

    _____ .

    a. strike while the iron is hot
    b. do as I say, not as I do
    c. leave well enough alone

II. Complete the dialogues with proverbs from the list below. Make changes in grammar and wording where needed.

an apple a day keeps the doctor away
do as I say, not as I do
if you can't beat them, join them
if you can't stand the heat, get out of the kitchen
leave well enough alone
look before you leap
make hay while the sun shines
strike while the iron is hot
the way to a man's heart is through his stomach
when in Rome do as the Romans do

Dialogue 1

Marta: Why are you making those brownies for Luís?

Jody: Can't you guess? _____ .
                        (The way to gain a man's love is by preparing food that he enjoys)

Marta: That may be true, but if you really love him you should give him healthy things to eat.

       You know, _____ .
                   (eating an apple every day helps a person to stay healthy)

Jody: I guess you're right. But didn't you give Bill a box of candy for his birthday last week?

Marta: Yes, I did. _____ .
                   (Follow my advice, but don't follow my example)

Dialogue 2

Libby: Why are you out of bed so early on your day off?

Reggie: I want to _____
(take advantage of an opportunity to do something)

The weather is good, so I'm going out to work in the yard.

Libby: The yard looks fine. Why don't you _____
(don't try to improve something that is already

_____ and relax today? We could go to the beach.
satisfactory)

Reggie: No, I need to cut the grass and pull some weeds.

Libby: Well, okay. _____ .
(If you can't defeat your opponents, join forces with them)

I'll come out and help you. When we're finished, maybe we can do something fun.

Dialogue 3

Raquel: I'm going to bet a hundred dollars on Lucky Louie to win.

Isaiah: You'd better _____ .
(consider all aspects of a situation before you take any action)

Can you really afford to lose that much money?

Raquel: I won't lose! I've won on the last three races, haven't I? I want to

_____ !
(act at the best possible time)

Isaiah: Your chances of winning aren't any better now than they ever are. It upsets me to see you throwing away so much money.

Raquel: Look, Isaiah. _____
(If you can't tolerate the pressures of a particular situation, remove yourself

_____ .
from that situation)

Isaiah: I think I will leave in a few minutes. But first I want to bet a few dollars on Smiling Sue.

After all, _____ .
(when traveling, follow the customs of the local people)

III. Fill in the blanks below, then find and circle the missing words in the puzzle. Be sure to look horizontally, vertically, and diagonally.

1. An apple a day keeps _____ away.

2. Do _____ , not as I do

3. If you can't beat them, _____ .

4. If you can't stand the heat, _____ .

5. Leave _____ alone.

6. Look before you _____ .

7. _____ while the sun shines.

8. Strike while _____ .

9. The way to _____ is through his _____ .

10. When in Rome _____ .

```
p  c  o  n  y  a  h  e  k  a  m  i  j  p  t  b  x  a  r  m  t
e  w  s  o  e  m  p  l  k  j  e  v  o  q  u  i  g  r  e  b  r
g  e  t  o  u  t  o  f  t  h  e  k  i  t  c  h  e  n  a  s  a
s  l  i  h  t  e  r  w  a  g  n  o  n  s  d  a  i  p  s  m  e
a  l  v  i  e  r  o  p  b  m  x  c  t  t  y  o  p  z  i  v  h
l  e  p  o  i  d  u  y  t  r  e  w  h  q  a  s  d  f  s  c  s
h  n  g  h  j  k  o  l  m  n  b  l  e  a  p  v  c  x  a  z  n
i  o  a  p  s  o  d  c  d  i  f  j  m  l  q  k  w  m  y  b  a
n  u  m  a  t  z  n  o  t  l  s  k  a  i  x  g  o  u  t  r  m
d  g  e  w  t  h  e  i  r  o  n  i  s  h  o  t  k  a  b  f  a
k  h  s  o  d  s  n  a  m  o  r  e  h  t  s  a  o  d  z  o  o
```

Answer Key

I. 1. a.   4. a.   7. a.   10. a.
    2. c.   5. c.   8. b.
    3. b.   6. c.   9. c.

II. **Dialogue 1**
The way to a man's heart is through his stomach; An apple a day keeps the doctor away; Do as I say, not as I do

Dialogue 2
make hay while the sun shines; leave well enough alone; If you can't beat them, join them

Dialogue 3
look before you leap; strike while the iron is hot; If you can't stand the heat, get out of the kitchen; when in Rome do as the Romans do

III. 1. the doctor   5. well enough   9. a man's heart, stomach
     2. as I say   6. leap   10. do as the Romans do
     3. join them   7. Make hay
     4. get out of the kitchen 8. the iron is hot

```
p  c  o  n  y  a  h  e  k  a  m  i  j  p  t  b  x  a  r  m  t
e  w  s  o  e  m  p  l  k  j  e  v  o  q  u  i  g  r  e  b  r
g  e  t  o  u  t  o  f  t  h  e  k  i  t  c  h  e  n  a  s  a
s  l  i  h  t  e  r  w  a  g  n  o  n  s  d  a  i  p  s  m  e
a  l  v  i  e  r  o  p  b  m  x  c  t  t  y  o  p  z  i  v  h
l  e  p  o  i  d  u  y  t  r  e  w  h  q  a  s  d  f  s  c  s
h  n  g  h  j  k  o  l  m  n  b  l  e  a  p  v  c  x  a  z  n
i  o  a  p  s  o  d  c  d  i  f  j  m  l  q  k  w  m  y  b  a
n  u  m  a  t  z  n  o  t  l  s  k  a  i  x  g  o  u  t  r  m
d  g  e  w  t  h  e  i  r  o  n  i  s  h  o  t  k  a  b  f  a
k  h  s  o  d  s  n  a  m  o  r  e  h  t  s  a  o  d  z  o  o
```

Section Three
Watch Out!

20.   All That Glitters Is Not Gold

Look before You Leap

Ask the class the following questions:

What is the tall man carrying? Can you describe it? What is he doing? What is his frame of mind? How can you tell? Can you guess why he might be feeling the way he does? How is he dressed? Judging from the appearance of his clothes, where in history would you place him? How about the little guy? Why do you think he is fleeing from the bigger guy? What could he have done to incur his wrath?

Make Hay While the Sun Shines

Ask the class the following questions:

For what purposes have swords been used during the course of history? Can you describe any incidents? Can you name other arms or implements that are used in battle? What are firearms? What are they made of? How do people use them? Has anybody ever tried to harm you for something you said or did? How? Describe the occasion. Have you ever deceived anyone? Why? Was it for your own personal gain, or was it for other, perhaps positive, reasons? Have you ever judged something simply by its appearance? Was your assessment justified? Describe a situation where such a judgment could be made. Do you think that something might have great value because it looks valuable? Describe instances where this might or might not be true. Do you think that something that is old and looks worn can be of any value? What in particular? How about personal belongings? What type of value do they have? For whom? What things that shine can be valuable? What things that shine can be of little or no value at all?

A Friend Who Shares . . .

Present this situation to the students for discussion:

A friend of yours is thinking about buying some stock in a company that produces and manufactures software for computers. The company has put out a glowing prospectus about current and projected sales. However, you find out that many complaints about the quality of the software have been registered with the Consumer Protection Agency. What would you tell your friend about this company if you want her to take a closer look before she invests?

Nothing Ventured, Nothing Gained

Have the students compose (orally or in writing) a speech or monologue based on the following situation:

Mark enjoyed browsing in old bookstores. One day he came across a book that appeared to be a first edition of a famous literary work. Although the book was selling for a fairly high price, he snapped it right up, thinking that the owner of the bookstore was not aware of its true value. Excitedly, he took the book to an expert to determine its true value. Much to Mark's dismay the book turned out to be a fake and was worth less than the price that he had paid for it.

21.   Curiosity Killed the Cat

Look before You Leap

Ask the class the following questions:

What does the mouse have in his hand? What is he about to do? Where is he? Can you describe what will happen? Who is peering into the hole? Why? What do you suppose he is trying to do? Why? Do you think that someone could get hurt? How? Does it appear that the cat is aware of the danger he is facing? Explain.

Make Hay While the Sun Shines

Ask the class the following questions:

The mouse is a rodent. Can you name other rodents? Do you know where different rodents live? Do you have any idea why they frighten people, especially women? Would you consider having a rodent as a pet? Why? Why not? Do you know what animals are the natural enemies of rodents? Can rodents be dangerous or cause problems for human beings? In what ways? Can you name and describe other types of cats? Where is their natural habitat? Are any type of cats dangerous to human beings? Do you know how cats protect themselves? Do they make good pets? Explain which one might and which ones might not. Why? In your opinion, is it natural to be curious? Do you think that curiosity is a positive trait? Explain why or why not. Can you name different situations that might incite one's curiosity? Has your curiosity ever gotten you into trouble? Describe the occasion. Can you think of occasions where it might pay to be curious?

A Friend Who Shares...

Present this situation to the students for discussion:

Your friend Nathan, an investigative reporter, has been trying to gather incriminating information for an exposé of a powerful local gangster. As his friend, you would do well to bring a certain fact to his attention. What would you say to him?

Nothing Ventured, Nothing Gained

Have the students compose (orally or in writing) a speech or monologue based on the following situation:

Gerald has been warned about keeping away from a secret government facility that is heavily guarded. The guards have orders to apprehend and detain any unauthorized person found within the parameters of the facility. Nevertheless, Gerald, curious about the projects being undertaken at the compound, keeps sneaking around, trying to penetrate the tight security so that he can find out what's going on.

22. Don't Bite Off More Than You Can Chew

Look before You Leap

Ask the class the following questions:

Can you describe the two animals in the picture? What is the smaller of the two trying to do? Why? Would you say that it is being successful? Why not? Do you think that it realizes the situation it is in? How is the larger of the two animals reacting? Does it seem concerned about its plight? Explain. Judging by the look in its eyes, what do you suppose it is thinking? Do you think it is in a position to turn the tables? Why? What do you imagine might eventually happen? Do you think that any harm can come to the smaller animal? How? Why?

Make Hay While the Sun Shines

Ask the class the following questions:

Snakes are reptiles. Can you name other reptiles? Can you describe some of them? Where are different types of reptiles usually found? Are they often not dangerous? For what reasons would a reptile attack another animal? How about a human being? What do reptiles usually eat? How do they stun their prey? Do you know if reptiles have teeth? How do they eat? Can you think of reasons why people fear reptiles? Have you ever been in a situation that you could not handle? Describe it. Do you consider yourself a responsible person? If so, have you ever assumed more responsibility than you could handle? Describe the situation. What was the outcome? Do you think that if you had accepted less responsibility you might have been more successful in accomplishing the task you had before you? Explain why or why not. For what reasons do you think a person would become involved in a project that he or she might not be able to complete? Why do you suppose that many people take on more work than they can reasonably handle?

A Friend Who Shares . . .

Present this situation to the students for discussion:

Mrs. Herrera is the mother of three children. She has been working in the office of her husband's clothing store and has been quite active in community affairs. She has just been asked to head a fund-raising committee for the purchase of a new wing for the local hospital. She is quite excited about the whole thing and comes to tell you of her intention to accept the responsibility. Being aware of her present commitments, what advice would you offer her?

Nothing Ventured, Nothing Gained

Have the students compose (orally or in writing) a speech or monologue based on the following situation:

Becky, a very bright and capable student, wants to finish high school in three years and start college—the sooner the better! She decides to take extra courses in evening school to complete the required curriculum. Alas! She finds that the load is too heavy for her. Her health begins to fail and her performance in day school begins to decline.

23.   Don't Bite the Hand that Feeds You

Look before You Leap

Ask the class the following questions:

What is the woman doing? What does she have around one of her hands? How do you imagine she is feeling? What do you think is wrong? What must have happened? How about the dog? How do you think it is feeling? Why? Does it look like the dog regrets what it did? What makes you think so? Where do you suppose it will go? Does the woman seem unforgiving? Why? Do you think she will let the dog come back? Why or why not?

Make Hay While the Sun Shines

Ask the class the following questions:

Do you know what insect is commonly found on dogs? What does it do to them? How do they react? Dogs are often called man's best friend. Why? Can you describe different breeds of dogs? Are they all friendly? Explain. Certain dogs are used to help human beings. Do you know which ones and how they help? The expression "dog eat dog" is often heard. Do you have any idea under what circumstances it might be used? When we say that someone or something has "gone to the dogs," do you know what we mean? Can you guess? Explain. Do you think that a dog might turn on its master? Why or why not? Under which circumstances might a dog attack a human being? In which profession do people complain most about being on their guard against dogs? Why do they complain? Have you ever done anyone a big favor? Explain. Were you repaid in any way? Did the person for whom you did a favor seem grateful? How did he or she express gratitude? Do you know of any occasions when someone has been ungrateful either to you or to someone else? Explain. How do you think that someone would react to gratitude or ingratitude? Can you cite any examples?

A Friend Who Shares... Present this situation to the students for discussion:

Vladimir felt sorry for Sergei when he came to him looking for a job. Although there were no openings, Vladimir offered his friend a position as a maintenance man. One day Vladimir asked his friend to make a deposit of the weekly receipts to the bank. Sergei left with the money, but instead of going to the bank he left town with it. He was finally apprehended by the authorities. Of course he lost his job and was jailed. What lesson did he learn?

Nothing Ventured, Nothing Gained Have the students compose (orally or in writing) a speech or monologue based on the following situation:

Your friend Ramón had once gotten in trouble for lying to his parents about his whereabouts on a particular night. He was very distraught and had come to stay with you until things settled down with his folks. You had taken care of his needs for food and shelter and had consoled him in the bargain. One day, when you yourself were in a situation where you needed his help, Ramón refused to have anything to do with you. His rejection hurt you a great deal.

24. Don't Count Your Chickens before They're Hatched

Look before You Leap Ask the class the following questions:

Where is the woman? What is she doing? How does she seem? Why? Who is there with her? Do you think he belongs there? How do you think he got there? What does he look like? Judging from his appearance, would you say that he was a welcome guest? Explain. Why is he remaining hidden? What do you think he will try to do when the woman leaves? Do you imagine he will be successful? Why or why not?

Make Hay While the Sun Shines Ask the class the following questions:

A chicken is an animal on a farm. Can you name other farm animals? What foods do these animals provide? Can you compare life on a farm with life in the city? Where would you rather live? Why? Can you name some advantages of living in the country? How about disadvantages? What are some advantages of living in a city? What are some of the disadvantages? What animals might harm the animals living on a farm? Why might they do this? Do farm animals make good pets? Which ones? Why? Which ones might not? Why? Have you ever planned on something that did not materialize? Explain. When you are planning an activity or project, does it usually turn out successfully? Explain. Do you believe that good, thorough planning for a project will guarantee its success? Explain why or why not. When something does not turn out for you, how do you feel? Are you discouraged from trying again? Can you recall a situation where you have counted on having something and then not gotten it? What happened?

A Friend Who Shares... Present this situation to the students for discussion:

A friend of yours who interviewed for a high corporate position has been talking about finally being able to buy that sports car he has been eyeing. Since he has not definitely been hired yet, what advice would you give him?

Nothing Ventured, Nothing Gained

Have the students compose (orally or in writing) a speech or monologue based on the following situation:

Vince has been working on a project for weeks now. His superiors have been very satisfied with his progress. Because of their constant support and praise, Vince can't help thinking that he will get a healthy bonus upon completion of the project.

25.   Don't Cry Over Spilt Milk

Look before You Leap

Ask the class the following questions:

What is the cat doing? What do you think happened? Why should the cat be so upset? Does it seem to you that what happened is something serious? Explain why or why not. What do you suppose was in the bottle? Do you think the cat is crying because it dropped the bottle? Explain. What do you suppose it would take to keep the cat from being so upset?

Make Hay While the Sun Shines

Ask the class the following questions:

How do cats show that they are content? How do they behave when they are angry? Do you think cats make good pets? Why or why not? Can you name other types of cats? Where are they found? Do you know what they eat? Do all cats like milk? In your opinion do all types of cats make good pets? Explain why or why not. In which ways are cats unique? How are they different from dogs? How do cats protect themselves? Do all cats protect themselves in the same ways? Can you describe the physical characteristics of cats in general? Do you believe that once something is done it cannot be undone? Explain why or why not. Have you ever done or said anything that you've regretted? What were the consequences? How did the situation eventually turn out? Were you able to make amends? Do you believe bad situations will eventually right themselves if you do nothing about them? Explain. What course of action do you think one should pursue when faced with a situation that has turned out badly? In your opinion, does it do any good to grieve about something that cannot be undone? Explain.

A Friend Who Shares...

Present this situation to the students for discussion:

Eric felt certain that he was going to get a superior grade in his history class. Unfortunately, because of his weak performance on his final exam, he received only an average grade for the course. Naturally, he felt terrible when he learned of the results, and he has not been able to shake off his disappointment. In this situation, what might one say to him?

Nothing Ventured, Nothing Gained

Have the students compose (orally or in writing) a speech or monologue based on the following situation:

The other day Jan made a phone call from a telephone booth. She took her wallet out of her purse to get some change for the call. In her haste to make the call, she left her wallet with all of her money and credit cards on a shelf under the phone. Upon completing the call, she hurriedly departed. When she was halfway home she suddenly remembered that she had left her wallet in the phone booth. When she got back to the booth to look for it, she could find no trace of her wallet. Of course, it had been stolen. Needless to say she was totally demoralized.

26. Don't Judge a Book by Its Cover

Look before You Leap

Ask the class the following questions:

What is the man doing with his glasses and outer garments? What type of outfit is he wearing underneath? Judging from his ordinary, everyday appearance, what type of person would you imagine he is? Why would you say so? What would the word "flash" indicate about the man? How about the bolt of lightning? Do you think the man might have more than one identity? Explain. If so, can you describe or contrast each one? If you had seen this man without his glasses on, could you have guessed that he might be just the opposite of what he appears to be? Explain your answer.

Make Hay While the Sun Shines

Ask the class the following questions:

Can you tell what a person is like by the way he or she looks or dresses. Why or why not? Can you describe different types of people? How do they behave? How do they dress? How do other people react to them? Have you ever met anyone who gave the impression of being a certain type of person, yet turned out to be just the opposite? Describe the occasion. Have you ever formed an opinion about someone based only on appearance? Were you justified in your opinion? Do you think that it is fair to judge a person by the way he looks? Why or why not? In your opinion, are appearances deceiving? Explain. Can you describe how you felt when you were wrong in your estimation of a person? In your opinion are first impressions valid? Why or why not? Do you think it is possible to keep from forming an opinion about someone when you first meet him or her? Explain. Name some traits in a person that you most admire. What traits do you find offensive? Can you say why?

A Friend Who Shares . . .

Present this situation to the students for discussion:

Dr. Hilderbrand had established a solid reputation as a psychologist in a quaint little town. However, one of his patients inadvertently discovered that the good doctor was a fugitive from justice and that he was wanted by the authorities for a number of illegal activities, including forgery and fraudulent practice of medicine. What do you imagine the inhabitants of the town would say about their assessment of the doctor?

Nothing Ventured, Nothing Gained

Have the students compose (orally or in writing) a speech or monologue based on the following situation:

When Dan came to his class reunion with a long ponytail and a leather jacket none of his former classmates could believe their eyes. When in high school Dan was always one of the most conservative students of the entire school. Everyone had thought he would eventually end up a lawyer or a corporate executive. Just imagine what everyone thought when he announced that he had formed a rock group and that he was soon going on a tour of the major cities of the United States and Europe!

27. Don't Judge a Man until You've Walked in His Boots

Look before You Leap

Ask the class the following questions:

Does it appear that the man is having a little trouble? What kind? Can you describe what he has on his feet? Would you say that they go with the rest of his outfit? Explain. Do you think that the man usually dresses in this fashion? If not, what would be different about the way he does dress? What reason could he possibly have for trying on something that clearly does not fit him? Do you think that the footwear belongs to him? Do you know who would wear the type of footwear depicted in the illustration? For what environment would it be appropriate? Explain.

Make Hay While the Sun Shines

Ask the class the following questions:

Can you name different kinds of footwear? For example, what do Eskimos wear? Why? What is their footwear made of? How about people who live in very hot climates? Can you describe the footwear of cowboys or American Indians? What is it made of? Why is it designed the way it is? How about people who hunt or fish? What type of footwear do they use? Do basketball players wear the same shoes as football or soccer players? What is the difference? Explain. How about gymnasts or track stars? Consider why certain types of footwear would or would not be suitable for certain climates, sports, or other activities. Can you name other articles of clothing that are suited to cold, temperate, or hot climates? Can you tell why? How about other articles of clothing for ordinary, formal, or professional wear? Can you name the type of clothing worn by athletes? Explain. Do you think it is possible to evaluate fairly another person's job or profession if you have never tried to do it yourself? In what instances might it be possible to do so? In what instances would it not be possible to do so? Have you ever had occasion to criticize another person? Can you recall the situation and tell why you did so? As you look back on the occasion, do you think that you had reason to criticize? Did you take into consideration all aspects of the situation before expressing your disapproval? Had you been in that person's position, do you think you could have done better? What would you have done differently and why? Do you think that your opinion would have been more valid and that you would understand the other person's position better if you had tried to do what he or she had done? Explain why or why not. Have you ever been criticized for the way you have done something? What was the occasion? Do you think that your performance was fairly evaluated? Tell why or why not.

A Friend Who Shares...

Present this situation to the students for discussion:

Christopher had complained to his brother Phillip about the performance of one of the players on his favorite football team. What would Phillip say to his brother if he thought that the criticism was not entirely justified?

Nothing Ventured, Nothing Gained

Have the students compose (orally or in writing) a dialogue based on the following situation:

Maurice had always been interested in music, although he had never played a musical instrument. After attending a jazz concert, he met with some musician friends in a coffeehouse and began discussing the concert. He thought that most of the players were quite good, except for the guy on the saxophone. He felt the saxophonist was lacking in originality and freshness of ideas in his improvisations. One of Maurice's musician friends reminded him that he would be in a better position to criticize if he, himself, knew more about the saxophone and about the difficulty of playing with a jazz combo.

28.   Don't Look a Gift Horse in the Mouth

Look before You Leap

Ask the class the following questions:

What is the man doing? Why? Who do you think he could be? Is he looking for something? What might it be? What does the horse have around its neck? Why? How do you think the horse feels? Explain. In your opinion is the procedure depicted in the illustration an ordinary one? Why or why not?

Make Hay While the Sun Shines

Ask the class the following questions:

Can you name other animals that are members of the horse family? Do you know what horses were used for in past times? Can you name, for instance, how horses have been used by soldiers? By cowboys? By farmers? In cities? For personal pleasure? For entertainment? Are certain horses more valuable than others? What makes them so? Mules and donkeys are like horses. What are they mainly used for? What reputation do they have? Can you think of what a horse might have in common with a llama or a camel? Where are llamas found? How are they used? How about camels? How are llamas, horses, and camels different from each other? Have you ever received a gift that you did not like? What was the occasion? How did you react? Did you accept it? Did you return it? Why? Do you think that a person should be grateful for a gift even if he or she doesn't like it? What type of gift has the most meaning for you? Why? How would you feel if it were brought to your attention that someone had complained about a gift that you had personally chosen for him or her? Under what circumstances do you think it would be okay to exchange a gift?

A Friend Who Shares...

Present this situation to the students for discussion:

Ryan's parents promised him a trip to New York if he finished the year with high grades. He finished at the top of his class, but when his parents presented him with the airline ticket he grumbled about the fact that it was only a coach-class and not a first-class ticket. What advice would you offer to him?

Nothing Ventured, Nothing Gained

Have the students compose (orally or in writing) a dialogue based on the following situation:

Molly's boyfriend knew she enjoyed symphonic music. One day he surprised her with a compact disc of a modern atonal work. However, when she saw who the composer was, she could not conceal her disappointment. She would have much preferred a symphony or a concerto by a composer of the romantic school of music.

29.   Don't Put All Your Eggs in One Basket

Look before You Leap

Ask the class the following questions:

What is the woman carrying? Is she having any problems? Why? What's happening? Why do you think she tried to carry everything all at once? How would she have been better off? Does it seem that she will reach her destination without further incident? Why or why not? What would you recommend that she do in order to avoid losing the rest of the contents of the basket?

Make Hay While the Sun Shines

Ask the class the following questions:

Can you name different ways in which eggs are prepared? What are some of your favorite egg dishes? Do you know if eggs are considered good for you? Eggs are often served with bacon. Do you know of any other meats that are served with eggs? How do you personally like your eggs? What other common dairy food is produced on a farm? What animal does it come from? Can you name other common farm animals? Do any of them make good pets? Explain why or why not. Eggs are often used in the preparation of pastry and other dishes. Can you name some of them? What ingredients are used in preparing them? Are you the type of person who takes risks? Explain. There are many types of risks. Can you name some of them? Are there any advantages to taking some of these risks? Explain. Do you know what a safe bet is? What type of people are inclined to make safe bets? What do you think it is better to do: invest all of your savings in one place with a chance of doubling your money quickly; or spread out your investments, although the yield is lower and slower? What are the advantages and disadvantages of either course of action?

A Friend Who Shares...

Present this situation to the students for discussion:

Your friend, Michael, has some money to invest. A stock broker has told him about a stock that is sure to double in value within a short time. He recommends that Michael invest all of his savings in the stock of this one company. What advice would you give to your friend?

Nothing Ventured, Nothing Gained

Have the students compose (orally or in writing) a speech or monologue based on the following situation:

Upon graduating from school, Lillian set her sights on a job with a particular company. She prepared her resumé and made an appointment for a job interview with one of the personnel officers of the company. Lillian felt so certain she would be hired that she did not even take the time to explore possibilities of employment elsewhere.

30. Don't Put Off for Tomorrow What You Can Do Today

Look before You Leap

Ask the class the following questions:

Where is the man going? How do you know? What is the condition of his car? How can you tell? From all appearances does it seem that the man will arrive at his destination? What makes you think the way you do? Can you describe the man and tell how he must be feeling? Would you say that he had any previous indications of trouble with his car? Explain the reasons for your opinion. Do you think that if the man had expected trouble he would have ventured to drive his car? What measures do you think he should have taken to ensure a safe, trouble-free ride?

Make Hay While the Sun Shines

Ask the class the following questions:

Can you describe some of the functions of an auto repair shop? What are the employees of the repair shop called? Can you name different kinds of cars? What type of person is most likely to buy a certain type of car? Do you know the names of the controls of a car? What features would you like to have on your personal car? What are the main safety features of a car? Do you like a standard or an automatic transmission? Why? How about air conditioning? What extras do you consider unnecessary? Do you think that a powerful motor is indispensable in a car? Why or why not? Can you say why certain people prefer to have a car that is capable of immediate high acceleration? Is this a dangerous thing? Explain. In your opinion who make the best drivers—men or women? Explain your point of view. Do you have a tendency to procrastinate? Do you think that many people are inclined to do so? Explain the reasons for your opinion. Why do you think people often postpone doing the things they should do? When a person says "I'll get to it," do you think that person more often than not neglects to take care of the matter? Can you recount such an occurrence from your own personal experience? Was the outcome positive or negative? If a person does not take care of a matter when he or she should, what could be some of the consequences of delay?

A Friend Who Shares . . .

Present this situation to the students for discussion:

Ray failed to send in his monthly bank loan payment on the due date. When he received his next month's statement he began complaining about the late charges that were added to his balance. What would you advise him to do in the future?

Nothing Ventured, Nothing Gained

Have the students compose (orally or in writing) a speech or monologue based on the following situation:

When Stephen was a senior in high school, he couldn't quite make up his mind about which college to attend. He finally decided on a small eastern university and obtained an application form for admission from his counselor, who advised him to fill it out and send it back right away. However, Stephen put the form aside "for the time being" because he felt that it was a bit too lengthy and required two or three written essays. When Stephen finally decided to complete the application he was greatly dismayed to learn that the application deadline for that particular college had already passed.

31. Don't Put the Cart before the Horse

Look before You Leap

Ask the class the following questions:

What is the horse doing? What kind of fruit do you think is in the cart? How is the cart attached to the horse? Do you have any idea as to why this might be so? Is this the normal way of harnessing a horse? If not, what is? What is the advantage of having the horse face the cart? How would you say the horse is feeling? Why?

Make Hay While the Sun Shines

Ask the class the following questions:

Do you know what a male horse is called? How about a female horse? What do horses normally eat? Can you name any different breeds of horses? Can you name different ways in which horses can be of service to man? Are you generally an organized person? Can you describe what an organized person is like? Have you ever done anything without considering all aspects of the outcome? Explain. Do you believe that doing things in the correct order will guarantee a successful outcome? Why? Do you think that doing a project out of order will necessarily lead to an unsuccessful outcome? Explain why or why not.

A Friend Who Shares . . .

Present this situation to the students for discussion:

Felicia has purchased an elegant dress for the senior prom. Although she is quite excited about the occasion, she has yet to be asked by any of her gentleman friends. What advice would you give her?

Nothing Ventured, Nothing Gained

Have the students compose (orally or in writing) a speech or monologue based on the following situation:

Jeffery knew that he needed a higher degree in business administration before he could obtain a coveted position with a particular business enterprise. Nevertheless, he applied for a low-level entry position, in the hopes of sliding in. Of course, he was quite upset when he was rejected. It was then that he decided he should go back to school to obtain the degree required for even minimal consideration of employment.

32.   A Miss Is As Good As a Mile

Look before You Leap

Ask the class the following questions:

Where is the man? Why do you imagine he's there? What is he holding in his hand? Can you describe the wheel in the illustration? Does it appear that the man has a good chance of winning some sort of prize? Explain. Would you say that the man is happy or disappointed? How can you tell? Why would he feel that way? From all appearances would you say that the man had reason to be hopeful about winning a prize? Explain.

Make Hay While the Sun Shines

Ask the class the following questions:

In your opinion, are most people inclined to gamble? Why or why not? What are the advantages? What are the disadvantages? What would you say is the motivating factor that would cause someone to take a risk? Can you name a situation where taking a risk has proved profitable? How about the opposite? What could be the consequences of losing? Can you name some games of chance? Can you describe them? Do you enjoy playing them? Why? Have you ever won any prizes or contests? If so, describe your experience. If not, have you ever been close to winning? Did you lose by a wide or narrow margin? Explain the situation. How did you feel? If you lost, did you lose your enthusiasm for trying one more time? What factors would make you try again? What factors would discourage you from persevering?

A Friend Who Shares . . .

Present this situation to the students for discussion:

Aaron has been talking to you about his performance in a national long-distance running competition. Although he sounded very excited over the fact that he came in one second under the world record, he feels that if he had tried just a little harder, he could not only have won the competition, but could have become world champion of the event as well. What would you say to him concerning his loss of the world championship?

Nothing Ventured, Nothing Gained

Have the students compose (orally or in writing) a speech or monologue based on the following situation:

Yesterday Natalie came home in tears. When her father asked why she was so upset, she told him that she was distraught over her final grade in her lit class. She needed an "A" in her final exam to get an "A" in the course. Unfortunately, she missed the "A" by two points!

33.   The Road to Hell Is Paved with Good Intentions

Look before You Leap

Ask the class the following questions:

Can you identify the two men in the illustration? How is the stout man dressed? What does he have over his eyes? What does this tell you about him? What objects are falling out of his coat? Where do you suppose he got them? Do you think he paid for them? Why do you think he is holding up his arms? What is he trying to communicate? Do you think he is happy about his destination? Why or why not? How about the other character? Can you describe him? To what place is he pointing? Judging from the look on his face, would you say that he is rejecting or welcoming the other man to his domain? Does it appear to you that the stout man can refuse to obey the other character? Does he have any choice? Explain.

Make Hay While the Sun Shines

Ask the class the following questions:

What is a sin? Can you name different sins? In what ways may people be punished for committing them? How would you define a religious person? Do religious people ever commit sins? What might make them do so? How do they atone for them? Can you name some of the main religions of the world? In what ways are they similar? In what ways do they differ? Do you personally believe in a superior force or being? If so, how does this belief influence your life? Do you think that people's behavior is at all influenced by fear of punishment? From what source? Would that source be a social institution or something else? What role do you think that conscience would play in influencing the behavior of a person? What factors can make a person misbehave or commit a crime? Do you think that some crimes are justified? Explain. In your opinion is it possible for one person to hurt another without intending to do so? Explain. What are procrastinators? Do you believe that they have put off the completion of a project on purpose, without any intention of following through? Explain why you believe as you do. When you make a promise, do you intend to keep it? If you don't keep your word, was it because you were not sincere? Do you believe you should be held accountable for not keeping your word? Explain.

A Friend Who Shares . . .

Present this situation to the students for discussion:

You and your friend Richard are watching a skydiving exhibition. Richard tells you that he's always been interested in skydiving but has yet to muster up the nerve to try it. Considering the fact that he has never followed through with his intention, what would you say to him?

Nothing Ventured, Nothing Gained

Have the students compose (orally or in writing) a speech or monologue based on the following situation:

Loretta does pretty well in all of her subjects except geometry. Her father, who is a math teacher, offered to tutor her. Unfortunately, every time she asks him to help her out with some proofs, he claims that he's either correcting papers or has some pressing engagement and cannot take the time to sit down and work with her. Although she doesn't say anything to her father about keeping his promise to help her with her homework, Loretta feels that he has let her down.

34.   Where There's Smoke, There's Fire

Look before You Leap

Ask the class the following questions:

What is the woman holding? What does the sign say? What's happening to the sign? Judging from what is written on the sign, do you suppose that everything is in order? If not, what could be the matter? Why would the woman be carrying the sign in the first place? What is the woman looking at? Does it appear that she is aware of what is happening? Explain. Do you suppose she is aware of a potential problem? What might make her think so?

Make Hay While the Sun Shines

Ask the class the following questions:

What does it mean "to be on strike"? What do people hope to accomplish by going on strike? Do you think that a group of workers can accomplish their goal by not reporting to work? What effect would a strike have on a particular enterprise? Have you ever been treated unfairly at work? If so, explain how. What did you do about it? Did you complain to your superior? What was his or her reaction? Did your complaint do any good? What—if anything—was done to improve the situation? Under what circumstances do you feel that it would be necessary to take matters into your own hands in order to change your situation? When you see or smell smoke, what do you think might be happening? In your opinion, is smoke necessarily an indication of a serious problem? Explain. Other than smoke, what indications would lead you to believe that something might be amiss? Can you recount a personal experience where you have had occasion to suspect that something might be wrong? What made you think so? How did you handle the situation? Do you often think there is a problem without really knowing why you think so? Have your suspicions been validated? Explain.

A Friend Who Shares . . .

Present this situation to the students for discussion:

Lately Pablo has been complaining of a gnawing pain in his lower back. In spite of the fact that the pain has been getting progressively worse, he has not gone to see his doctor to check it out. You feel that he is wrong to let it go and that he ought to seek medical advice to determine the cause of the pain. What could you say to him in order to get him to go see his doctor?

Nothing Ventured, Nothing Gained

Have the students compose (orally or in writing) a dialogue based on the following situation:

Before leaving the house to visit her daughter, Mrs. Cheng had opened the bedroom drapes and turned the lights on. After their visit, as they were returning to their home, the Chengs noted that the bedroom was dark, and that the drapes were drawn. They immediately suspected that a robbery must have occurred during their absence. Not wanting to take any chances on being surprised by a burglar, Mr. Cheng decided to stop the car and call the police before he and his wife entered the house.

Practice Makes Perfect

I.   Complete the sentences with proverbs from the list below. Make changes in grammar and wording where needed.

all that glitters is not gold
curiosity killed the cat
don't bite off more than you can chew
don't bite the hand that feeds you
don't count your chickens before they're hatched
don't cry over spilt milk
don't judge a book by its cover
don't judge a man until you've walked in his boots
don't look a gift horse in the mouth
don't put all your eggs in one basket
don't put off for tomorrow what you can do today
don't put the cart before the horse
a miss is as good as a mile
the road to hell is paved with good intentions
where there's smoke, there's fire

1.   —That new history teacher looks really mean. I hope I don't have a class with him.

     —_____ . I heard he has a great sense of humor.

2.   —Did you see the Bulls game last night? I couldn't believe they lost by one point at the buzzer.

     —Yes, it was too bad they broke their winning streak. Unfortunately, _____ .

3.   —I'm sorry I ruined your new blouse, Sandy. I just wanted to help you out by doing the laundry.

     —I understand, Chris. But _____ . Next time, ask me how you can help.

4.   —Why are you opening that letter? It's addressed to Myrna.
     —I know. It's from Dan. I want to know what's going on between them.

     —You shouldn't read other people's mail. It's not nice. Besides, _____ .
5.   —How was the concert last night? Did Vince do a good job on his solo?
     —I didn't think it was too great. I don't know why everyone thinks he's such a good violinist.

     —Maybe that's because you've never tried to play the violin. _____ !

6.   —Did you write your book report, Keith?
     —No, but it's not due until Friday. I have plenty of time.

     —_____ . I want you to write the book report before you watch TV.

7. —Did you apply for the job at Garcia's Market, Frank?
   —No. I already applied at Sam's Video.

   —I think you should apply for more than one job. _____ .

8. —I'm going to buy a new car tomorrow.
   —Really? Do you have enough money?
   —Not yet, but I bought a lottery ticket and I feel lucky.
   —I don't think it's a good idea to spend money before you have it. Remember,

   _____ .

9. —You look upset, Carla. Is something wrong?
   —Yes! I bought a VCR at a garage sale yesterday. It was all clean and shiny and looked great. But when I got home, I found out that it didn't work.

   —I'm sorry to hear that, but you should know that _____ .

10. —I see you're wearing new PowerGlide tennis shoes!
    —They're not new. My brother gave them to me. You can see that they are dirty and the soles are worn.

    —_____ . Be happy to have PowerGlides!

11. —I saw Elmer talking to the security officer this morning. I think there must be some trouble in the computer center.
    —Just because someone talks to the security officer doesn't mean that there is trouble.

    —Maybe not, but usually _____ .

12. —I hope Emilio likes living here in Oregon. I want to stay here after we get married.
    —Did he ask you to marry him?
    —No.

    —Then I wouldn't worry about leaving Oregon. _____ .

13. —Here, I'll type up that contract for you.
    —But Kenyatta, you already have the other contracts to type, and you have a client coming at

    3:00. _____ .

14. —Ms. Zephyr offered to increase my salary if I quit my job at Zinkel's and go to work for her.
    —Mr. Zinkel gave you a job when you really needed one, and he treats you very well. He will feel

    hurt if you quit. _____ .

15. —I feel so bad. I accidentally washed the painting Jordan made for me at nursery school. It's ruined!

    —_____ . I'm sure Jordan will paint more pictures for you.

II.   Match the situation in column A with the proverb in column B.

A   **B**

_____ 1. Stop poking your nose into other   a. All that glitters is not gold.
              people's business.

_____ 2. That painting may not be worth   b. Where there's smoke, there's fire.
              $400.

_____ 3. I know you just want to help me,   c. Don't look a gift horse in the mouth.
              but don't lie about what happened.

_____ 4. Sam may seem unreasonable, but   d. Don't bite off more than you can chew.
              he has a difficult job.

_____ 5. I'll get those insurance forms filled e. Remember, curiosity killed the cat!
              out tomorrow.

_____ 6. Why are you complaining? The   f. Don't cry over spilt milk.
              software was free.

_____ 7. I was one of the final candidates   g. The road to hell is paved with good intentions.
              for the job, but I didn't get it.

_____ 8. You'd better wait until you get that   h. Don't put off for tomorrow what you can do
              raise before buying a CD player.   today.

_____ 9. Why are you buying a lawn trac-   i. Don't judge a man until you've walked in his
              tor? You haven't bought a house   boots.
              yet.

_____ 10. Are you sure you can handle the   j. Don't count your chickens before they're
              extra work?   hatched.

_____ 11. The salesperson was very hand-   k. A miss is as good as a mile.
              some and well dressed.

_____ 12. I'm sorry you broke that vase, but   l. Don't put all your eggs in one basket.
              we can't do anything about it now.

_____ 13. Tommy has chocolate on his face.   m. Don't bite the hand that feeds you.
              Do you think he got into the cook-
              ies again?

_____ 14. I don't think you should put all   n. Don't put the cart before the horse.
              your money in one stock.

_____ 15. Ms. Garcia pays your salary. Don't   o. Don't judge a book by its cover.
              tell stories about her.

III. Complete the crossword puzzle using the clues below.

Across

1. don't bite off more than you can _____

2. don't count your chickens before they're _____

7. don't judge a book by its _____

11. don't look a _____ in the mouth

12. the road to hell is paved with good _____

13. don't cry over _____

14. where there's _____ , there's fire

Down

1. _____ killed the cat

3. don't put off for _____ what you can do today

4. all that _____ is not gold

5. don't put the _____ before the horse

6. a miss is as good as a _____

8. don't put all your _____ in one basket

9. don't _____ the hand that feeds you

10. don't judge a man until you've walked in his _____

Answer Key

I.   1. Don't judge a book by its cover.

2. a miss is as good as a mile.

3. the road to hell is paved with good intentions.

4. curiosity killed the cat.

5. Don't judge a man until you've walked in his boots!

6. Don't put off for tomorrow what you can do today.

7. Don't put all your eggs in one basket.

8. don't count your chickens before they're hatched.

9. all that glitters is not gold.

10. Don't look a gift horse in the mouth.

11. where there's smoke, there's fire.

12. Don't put the cart before the horse.

13. Don't bite off more than you can chew.

14. Don't bite the hand that feeds you.

15. Don't cry over spilt milk.

II.   1. e.   6. c.   11. o.

2. a.   7. k.   12. f.

3. g.   8. j.   13. b.

4. i.   9. n.   14. l.

5. h.   10. d.   15. m.

III.

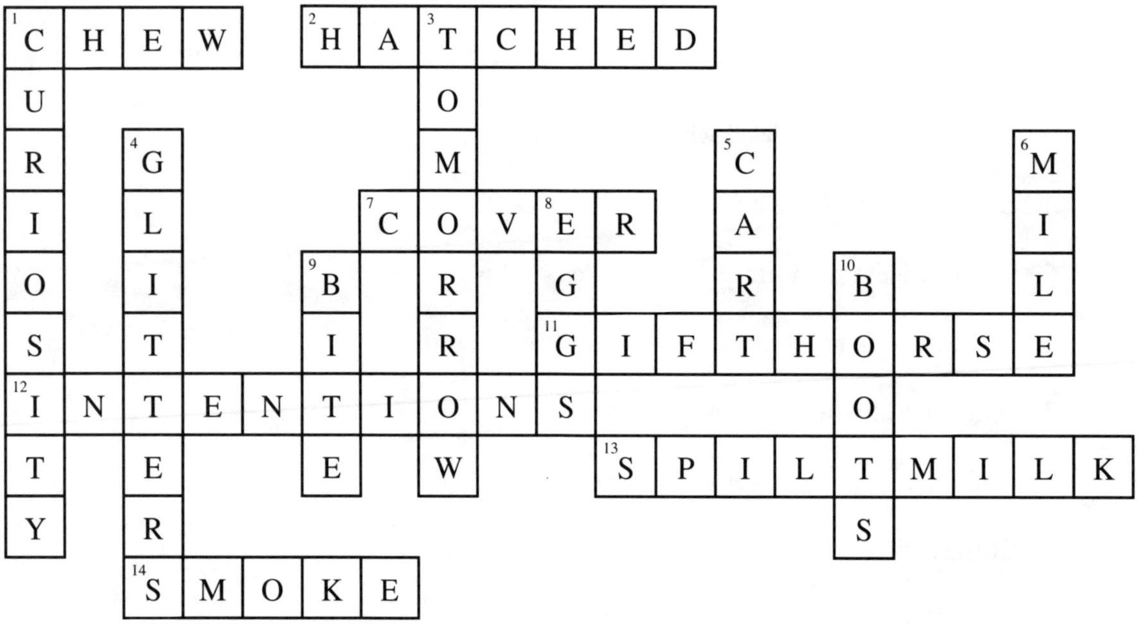
1 CHEW
2 HATCHED
3 TOMORROW
1 CURIOSITY
4 GLITTER
5 CART
6 MILE
7 COVER
8 EGGS
9 BITE
10 BOOTS
11 GIFTHORSE
12 INTENTIONS
13 SPILTMILK
14 SMOKE

Section Four
Getting Ahead

35.   The First Step Is Always the Hardest

Look before You Leap

Ask the class the following questions:

Where is the woman in the illustration? What is she stepping on? What do you suppose she is trying to do? Does it look like she is experiencing some kind of difficulty? How can you tell? Would you say that the woman is confident that she will be successful in reaching her destination? If so, what makes you think so? If not, what makes you think not? What do you think will happen if the woman loses her footing? Judging from the illustration, would you say that she is in any kind of danger? Why or why not? Does it appear that she will reach her destination if she gets past the first stone?

Make Hay While the Sun Shines

Ask the class the following questions:

Have you ever taken a dare? If so, describe the circumstances. What were your feelings before attempting to fulfill the conditions of the challenge? Were you successful? Did you have to try again? Was it difficult to proceed? Do you have tendency to avoid doing certain things? If so, is it because of fear or inexperience, or is it because you simply do not want to face doing something that will consume a great deal of your time? Once you embark on a project, do you see it through? What factors would make you continue to pursue your goal in spite of difficulties? What factors might discourage you? Do you believe that once you begin doing something, it will be relatively easy to finish it? Explain. In your opinion is it harder to begin doing something or is it harder to accomplish what you set out to do? Explain why you feel as you do.

A Friend Who Shares...

Present this situation to the students for discussion:

Sean has been smoking for many years and had never thought about giving it up until his doctor told him that he was seriously endangering his health. Of course, Sean's worried that he won't be able to stop and hasn't been able to bring himself to make a concerted effort to do so. What could you tell him to get him to make an effort to drop the habit?

Nothing Ventured, Nothing Gained

Have the students compose (orally or in writing) a speech or monologue based on the following situation:

Mrs. Pappas got an expensive personal computer from her family to facilitate the accounting and paperwork of her new business. Although she appreciated the gift, she hesitated to set it up because she feared that she would never be able to learn how to use it. However, at the insistence of her family, Mrs. Pappas finally got down to reading the user's manual, and much to her surprise she discovered that the computer was relatively simple to operate and that she easily would be able to learn to program it to fit her business needs.

36.   Forewarned Is Forearmed

Look before You Leap

Ask the class the following questions:

Can you describe the two men in the illustration? What type of hat is each wearing? What do their hats tell you about their professions? What symbol is on the front of each hat? What do you suppose it means? What does one of the men have around his neck? What is this a part of? What does the other man have over his eye? Can you describe the rest of his appearance? Does it appear that he could be trusted? Why or why not? What do you think the little bird is trying to say? Why? Does it appear that the sailor will have a safe voyage? What dangers might he encounter?

Make Hay While the Sun Shines

Ask the class the following questions:

Can you name different types of sailing vessels? In what circumstances or for what purpose are they used? In past years what dangers did vessels face on the high seas? Do they face the same dangers nowadays? Explain. What is a pirate? Why were pirates feared? What did pirates often do with their plunder? Have you ever been caught by surprise? Can you describe the occasion? How did you react? How did things turn out? Do you think you might have been able to avoid problems had you known what was going to happen? Would you have taken another course of action? What would you have done? Do you think people usually heed the advice of others? Explain under what circumstances they might or might not. Do you think it is always possible to avoid catastrophe if you know about it in advance? Explain. If the catastrophe cannot be totally avoided, can it at least be minimized? Can you think of situations where advance warning might not minimize tragedy?

A Friend Who Shares...

Present this situation to the students for discussion:

Philip had been coming late to work. His supervisor let Philip's friend Marc know that he planned to dismiss Philip if he continued to be tardy. Marc immediately went to Philip and informed him of his conversation with the supervisor. What was Marc thinking of when he went to see his friend?

Nothing Ventured, Nothing Gained

Have the students compose (orally or in writing) a dialogue based on the following situation:

Mr. Voronov had had a bad day at work and came home early. His son Andrei had made a date for that night and planned to ask his father to borrow the car. When Andrei got home after school he mentioned his plans to his mother. Of course, Mrs. Voronov knew that her husband was feeling out of sorts and informed her son of this fact before he approached his father.

37.   He Who Hesitates Is Lost

Look before You Leap

Ask the class the following questions:

Where is the man standing? Why do you think he won't jump? What is the name of the animal behind him? What do you think will happen to the man if he doesn't jump? How about the woman? What did she do? Can you compare her course of action with that of the man? What character trait does the man lack? What quality of character is shown by the woman?

Make Hay While the Sun Shines

Ask the class the following questions:

Can you name other animals that have horns? In what natural habitat do they live? Are they usually aggressive? If so, explain under what circumstances. Have you ever hesitated to take a particular course of action? Describe the situation. Do you believe that acting decisively in a given situation will ensure a successful outcome? Why or why not? Would you have been better off had you not acted decisively? In your opinion what factors might ensure the successful outcome of a given course of action?

A Friend Who Shares...

Present this situation to the students for discussion:

Kenji has just informed his friend Ito that he was successful in obtaining a ticket for an upcoming rock concert. He went on to explain that tickets were going fast. Kenji knows that his friend would very much like to attend. What advice would Kenji give to his friend?

Nothing Ventured, Nothing Gained Have the students compose (orally or in writing) a speech or monologue based on the following situation:

Nadine, a rather shy young lady, has been standing on her feet all day long at work. It's finally quitting time and she leaves to catch a bus for home. It is the height of the rush hour and busses are usually crowded at this time. When Nadine gets on the bus along with several people, she notices that there is an empty seat toward the back. She thinks that this is one time when she has to overcome her shyness and act agressively.

38. If at First You Don't Succeed, Try, Try Again

Look before You Leap Ask the class the following questions:

Who is the woman in the illustration? How is she dressed? Why would she be dressed this way? In what athletic activity is she engaged? Does it appear that she has been doing well? Explain. From all appearances would you say that she is discouraged from continuing the race? Can you explain why she might want to continue?

Make Hay While the Sun Shines Ask the class the following questions:

Can you name other athletic events? Which ones appeal to you? Do you engage in any sports? Which ones? Are you proficient? How did you achieve your proficiency? Have you ever been discouraged from achieving a certain goal? What factors might make you want to go on? What factors might make you stop trying? Explain. Do you believe that it is possible to achieve success in a particular venture if you try hard enough? Explain why or why not. Do you believe that success inevitably comes to those who try hard enough? What other things, besides effort, help to ensure success in the achievement of a particular goal?

A Friend Who Shares... Present this situation to the students for discussion:

You have just met your friend Sharon for lunch. While the two of you are conversing Sharon expresses her disappointment over the fact that she was not selected as one of the members of the school debating team. What advice would you give her?

Nothing Ventured, Nothing Gained Have the students compose (orally or in writing) a speech or monologue based on the following situation:

Noreen has always dreamed of becoming a lawyer. After completing a number of courses at the university, she applied for law school and after two years of intensive study she took the bar exam. Unfortunately, her name did not appear on the list of those who passed. Needless to say, she was devastated. But she was not deterred. She decided to attend a number of review seminars and take the test again.

39. Necessity Is the Mother of Invention

Look before You Leap Ask the class the following questions:

Can you describe the scene in the illustration? What is standing on one side of the ledge? What is between the two ledges? With what situation was the woman faced? What did she have to do? Do you think that the woman would have been able to get to the other ledge by jumping? Why or why not? How did she finally manage to get to the other side? Can you think of any other way she might have been able to get there? If so, describe it.

Make Hay While the Sun Shines

Ask the class the following questions:

Do you know the names of any trees? Can you describe some of them? Where do they grow? In which ways do they benefit us? Have you ever been faced with a problem that you could not solve? Explain. What did you try to do to solve it? Were you successful the first time? If not, what course of action did you take? Describe. Do you believe that there can be a solution to any problem if a person is creative enough? Why or why not?

A Friend Who Shares . . .

Present this situation to the students for discussion:

Carla and Monique were driving home from a school function when all of a sudden they heard a small explosion and the car started to weave. They realized that they had a flat tire and pulled off to the side of the road. There was a spare in the trunk, but neither Carla nor Monique had ever changed a flat tire before. They knew that they would have to be resourceful. What might one of the girls have said to the other as they were getting out of the car to replace the flat with the spare?

Nothing Ventured, Nothing Gained

Have the students compose (orally or in writing) a speech or monologue based on the following situation:

Bjorn felt that it was time to have his house painted. Since he had never had the occasion to do any painting at all, he went out and got several estimates for the job. The estimates proved too high for his budget. He realized that if the job were to be done, he would have to learn to do it himself.

40. No Pain No Gain

Look before You Leap

Ask the class the following questions:

What is the woman doing in the illustration? What's at the top of the mountain? Does it appear that it would be easy to reach the top? Why do you suppose that the woman is trying so hard to get to the top? Does it all seem worth the effort? Why?

Make Hay While the Sun Shines

Ask the class the following questions:

Have you ever tried to climb a mountain? Do you imagine that it would be easy or difficult to do? Why? Have you ever strived to achieve something? Can you describe the situation? Do you think that most things can be achieved without effort? Why or why not? Do you have any special talents? Describe them. Do certain things come easy to you? Describe them. Is there something you would like to accomplish but have avoided because of the difficulty involved? Comment on the situation.

A Friend Who Shares . . .

Present this situation to the students for discussion:

Derrick had always been rather frail, and as he got older he decided to take up weight lifting to develop his muscles and add more definition to his body. What do you suppose Derrick told himself—knowing that it would take hard work to achieve his goal?

Nothing Ventured, Nothing Gained

Have the students compose (orally or in writing) a speech or monologue based on the following situation:

Since childhood, Jean-Paul had had a special talent for painting. He underwent many hardships to develop his gift. In spite of the fact that he had had a number of exhibitions of his paintings, he had not achieved recognition as an outstanding artist of his generation. Nevertheless, he was patient and kept working hard at his art, for he realized that the road to fame would not be an easy one.

41.   Nothing Ventured, Nothing Gained

Look before You Leap

Ask the class the following questions:

Where are the two men? Can you describe the setting? What is swimming in the water? Can you describe the man on the left? How is he dressed? What is he carrying? What do you suppose he is trying to do? Why? How about the man on the right? In which ways are his circumstances different? Make a comparison of the two.

Make Hay While the Sun Shines

Ask the class the following questions:

Can you name some creatures of the sea? Can you describe any of them? Which ones are dangerous to man? Which ones are used as food for man? Can you think of any occasions where a person might be successful without having tried to achieve that success? Do you think that if a person really tries hard, success is sure to follow? Explain why you feel as you do. If it appears that someone has little or no chance of achieving a goal, should he or she give up trying? How about you? Have you ever failed to obtain something you wanted? Did you refuse to try because the situation seemed hopeless? Describe the circumstances. Can you describe a hopeless situation where things unexpectedly turned out well for you because you made an effort to succeed?

A Friend Who Shares...

Present this situation to the students for discussion:

Although Alex is a gifted actor, he is hesitant to audition for a new Broadway musical because he lacks dance skills. You are convinced that he would get a part if he would only try out. What advice would you give to Alex?

Nothing Ventured, Nothing Gained

Have the students compose (orally or in writing) a dialogue based on the following situation:

All through school Drew had had trouble with his studies; however, he had a great desire to follow in his father's footsteps. His father was a pilot for one of the big commercial airlines. After Drew completed high school, his father offered to pay for his tuition and living expenses at a renowned pilot training school. Much to his father's chagrin, Drew vacillated in accepting the offer. When asked why, Drew explained that he was afraid that he would not be able to complete the course successfully and therefore did not even want to try. His father, however, remained adamant and told his son he should at least make the effort.

42.   The Pen Is Mightier Than the Sword

Look before You Leap

Ask the class the following questions:

What are the two women doing? What does each one have in her hand? One of the women seems to be having some trouble. Can you tell why? Which one of the two implements seems able to inflict the most harm? Which of the two women seems to have the upper hand? Would you say that this is because of her agility and skill? Explain why you feel as you do.

Make Hay While the Sun Shines

Ask the class the following questions:

The sword is an implement. Can you think of other implements that have a cutting edge? For what purposes are they used? The pen is a writing implement. In what way do you think that a pen can be mightier than a sword? Can you name some ways in which conflicts can be resolved? Do you think that the use of force is sometimes needed to solve a dispute? Explain why or why not. In what other ways can disputes be solved? In your opinion, which ways are the most effective? Explain. Have you ever had to resort to force to resolve a conflict? Were you successful? Explain the circumstances. Would another course of action have been just as effective? Do you believe that "might makes right"? In which ways can the written word be more powerful than physical force?

A Friend Who Shares...

Present this situation to the students for discussion:

Eric informs you that he intends to have a fight with one of his classmates after school because the classmate made abusive remarks to him during a break between classes. You tell Eric that a fight would only lead to more trouble. A letter to the principal of the school would be much more effective. What could you say to him that might make him change his mind?

Nothing Ventured, Nothing Gained

Have the students compose (orally or in writing) a speech or monologue based on the following situation:

Isaac formed a committee to help renovate an old building in his neighborhood for use as a youth center. The city planning commissioner, however, opposed the idea and refused to grant permission for the work. Some of the members of Isaac's committee became so angry at hearing the bad news that they began talking about the use of physical force to convince the commissioner to change his mind. Isaac, of course, rejected this idea and instead appealed in writing directly to the mayor of the city. After reading how the youth center would offer constructive programs to help keep the neighborhood children out of trouble, the mayor overrode the commissioner and granted permission to proceed with the renovation.

43. Practice Makes Perfect

Look before You Leap

Ask the class the following questions:

What is the woman holding? Can you describe how she is dressed? What is she doing? Does it appear that she is good at what she is doing? Why or why not? What is on the ground? What does this indicate? In view of what the woman is doing, would you say that her skill might improve? On what do you base your opinion?

Make Hay While the Sun Shines

Ask the class the following questions:

Many sports require special uniforms or outfits. Can you describe some of them and tell why they are worn for a particular sport? Can you name some sports in which some type of ball is used? Do you know the difference between an amateur player and a professional player? How does one reach the status of a professional player? What must one to do improve one's skill in any activity requiring coordination of mind and body? Why? Do you have any abilities in a particular sport? Describe. What must you do to maintain your level of performance? What happens if you don't stay with it? Do you believe that anyone can achieve a high level of performance in a sport if that person keeps trying to improve and does not allow himself or herself to be discouraged by failure? Explain why you feel as you do.

A Friend Who Shares...

Present this situation to the students for discussion:

Tod runs into his friend Edmond and tells him that he will be competing in a major golf tournament. Edmond congratulates his friend and praises him for having acquired the skill to compete with the professionals. What would Tod say about how he developed the skill to compete on such a high level?

Nothing Ventured, Nothing Gained

Have the students compose (orally or in writing) a speech or monologue based on the following situation:

Gallina had always excelled in foreign languages. She had been raised trilingual, and her goal was to become a translator. As she matured she unceasingly nurtured her language skills by reading foreign literature and by associating with native speakers through travel and residence in foreign countries. Gallina's skills were of such a high caliber that she had no problem obtaining an important position as a translator for the United Nations!

44. Rome Wasn't Built in a Day

Look before You Leap

Ask the class the following questions:

Who are the men in the illustration? How are they dressed? What period of history are they from? What are they carrying? Would you say that the men are having some difficulty carrying it? Why? Of what material do you suppose it is made? What would be the advantage of using such a material?

Make Hay While the Sun Shines

Ask the class the following questions:

Can you describe any aspects of Roman architecture? Can you compare Roman architecture with Greek architecture? Were they similar? Could one be an imitation of the other? If so, in what way? In view of the Mediterranean climate, can you comment on the form or style of houses in which the Romans lived? Do you think it took a long time to construct a Roman temple or residence? Explain your views. How about the architecture in your native country? Can you describe the buildings or type of housing typical of your country? What materials are used in construction? Why? What are the advantages or disadvantages of using such materials? How do you think modern architecture compares with the architecture of the Roman empire? Is one type better or more lasting than the other? Explain your answer. Do you think it is possible to put lasting quality into a hastily constructed structure? State reasons for your opinion. When you are working on a project, do you usually take your time? Why? Do you think it is possible to get a good command of a subject or discipline if you must accomplish it under pressure? Name some instances where it would be possible and some where it would not.

A Friend Who Shares . . . Present this situation to the students for discussion:

Your parents have been nagging you to quit smoking. You have agreed to do so, but in stages. They realize that you have not yet quit completely, and they are becoming impatient with you. What do you say to them to help justify your plan?

Nothing Ventured, Nothing Gained Have the students compose (orally or in writing) a dialogue based on the following situation:

Adrian had contracted to do a translation of an important foreign novel. He was going along at a moderate pace when one day he received a phone call from one of the editors who informed him that the demand for the novel's translation was so great that the date of publication had been moved up six months. Adrian felt overwhelmed and reminded the editor that an authoritative translation takes time.

45. The Squeaking Wheel Gets the Oil

Look before You Leap Ask the class the following questions:

Where are the two women? What is the woman on the left doing? How does she seem? Is she calm? What do you suppose she wants? Why would she be waving her hand? Does it seem like something is wrong? Who is approaching her? Does the woman on the right also want his attention? How is she trying to get it? Can you compare the behavior of the two ladies? Which one is the most aggressive? Which one do you think will get waited on first? Why?

Make Hay While the Sun Shines Ask the class the following questions:

Are there any good foreign restaurants in your city? If so, describe one. In your opinion what factors should be considered in judging the excellence of a restaurant? Would you like to work at a restaurant job? Why or why not? Have you ever had a negative experience in a restaurant? What were the circumstances? How was it resolved? Do you think it does any good to complain about something? Why or why not? How do you react when someone shouts at you? Do you do what they ask of you or do you turn the other way? If you were in a position where you waited on customers, would you naturally give more attention to someone who clamored for your attention or would you ignore that person? Explain how you would handle the situation. What would you do or say if an employee passed you by for service when it was your turn to be served?

A Friend Who Shares . . . Present this situation to the students for discussion:

A couple walked into a restaurant and after being seated they demanded to be served right away, as they were in a hurry to get to an important engagement. The waiter immediately placed their order with the cook. The couple at the adjoining table who had arrived ten minutes earlier overheard the conversation. What do you suppose ran through their minds?

Nothing Ventured, Nothing Gained Have the students compose (orally or in writing) a dialogue based on the following situation:

Jeanette and Jaime usually share their toys and play well together. However, at times they both want to play with the same toy and start quarreling over it. On such occasions their mother usually steps in and ends up by giving the toy to the one who cries loudest.

46. You're Never Too Old to Learn

Look before You Leap

Ask the class the following questions:

Can you describe the woman in the illustration? About how old would you say she is? What type of outfit is she wearing? What instrument is she playing? What is she wearing on her feet? What is attached to her heels? Does it appear that the woman is frail and demure? Explain why or why not. What type of music do you think she is playing? What makes you think so? Why do you suppose the instrument is attached to such a large speaker? Does it seem to you that she has been playing this type of music all her life? Explain why you think as you do.

Make Hay While the Sun Shines

Ask the class the following questions:

Can you name other stringed instruments? How are they played? Are they all played the same way? Which ones might be heard more often in a symphonic orchestra? Which ones would be heard more often in a rock or jazz group? Do you happen to know what the sections of the orchestra are? Can you name some instruments in each? Do you think that some stringed instruments are harder to play than others? Which ones? Why? Do you play an instrument? Which one? Did you start studying at an early age? Were you interested in learning or were you prodded to do so by your parents? Do you think it is possible to learn to play a musical instrument at an older age? Why or why not? Have you ever tried to acquire a new skill? Describe the occasion. Was it relatively easy or difficult to do so? Did you keep it up? Why or why not? Do you know of anybody who has tried to acquire a new skill at a more advanced age? Was it easy or difficult for them to do so? Explain.

A Friend Who Shares...

Present this situation to the students for discussion:

Angela had married at an early age. Now that her children were grown and out on their own, she decided to do something she had always wanted to do—become a belly dancer! What does this serve to prove?

Nothing Ventured, Nothing Gained

Have the students compose (orally or in writing) a dialogue based on the following situation:

It's been many years since you've seen your friend Bart. You happen to bump into him at an art exhibition and much to your amazement you discover that the works on exhibit are his! You're pretty surprised to see your friend in the role of artist because he spent most of his life as an accountant in a business firm.

Practice Makes Perfect

I.   Select the best proverb to complete each paragraph. In some cases, more than one answer is possible.

1. I know you are tired, but you only have twenty more push-ups to do. _____
    a. Rome wasn't built in a day.
    b. No pain, no gain.
    c. The squeaking wheel gets the oil.

2. Maria wants to get her GED, but she's afraid to go back to school. I told her to go ahead and call

    the college. _____
    a. The first step is always the hardest.
    b. Practice makes perfect.
    c. Necessity is the mother of invention.

3. If you play your flute for an hour every day, you'll be ready for the recital. _____
    a. Practice makes perfect.
    b. You're never too old to learn.
    c. Forewarned is forearmed.

4. Emily is investing in Frank's new restaurant. She hopes that the restaurant will be successful and

    that she will make some money on her investment. _____
    a. The pen is mightier than the sword.
    b. Practice makes perfect.
    c. Nothing ventured, nothing gained.

5. Kyoko is worried because her company isn't making much of a profit. I told her that it takes time

    for a new company to make a profit. After all, _____ .
    a. Rome wasn't built in a day
    b. you're never too old to learn
    c. he who hesitates is lost

6. Alberto said that he just couldn't understand algebra. I told him to work on it some more.

    _____
    a. The pen is mightier than the sword.
    b. If at first you don't succeed, try, try again.
    c. He who hesitates is lost.

7. When you meet with the loan officer, be sure to take some proof of your income. That will make

    the application process go more smoothly. _____
    a. Necessity is the mother of invention.
    b. No pain, no gain.
    c. Forewarned is forearmed.

8. If Mr. Lowe offers you the chance to represent the company in France, take it! If you turn it

   down, you may never get another chance. _____
   a. Practice makes perfect.
   b. He who hesitates is lost.
   c. The squeaking wheel gets the oil.

9. I told Ralph that he should write a letter of complaint to the company instead of threatening to

   punch the salesman. _____
   a. Nothing ventured, nothing gained.
   b. The first step is always the hardest.
   c. The pen is mightier than the sword.

10. My grandfather just started to take piano lessons. Oh well, _____.
    a. Rome wasn't built in a day
    b. you're never too old to learn
    c. forewarned is forearmed

11. Molly developed that CatPole to keep her cat from scratching her new sofa. Now Molly is selling

    about a hundred CatPoles a week! I guess it is true that _____ .
    a. the squeaking wheel gets the oil
    b. the first step is always the hardest
    c. necessity is the mother of invention

12. I complained to the janitor every day for two weeks, and I finally got a new screen in my window.

    Sara still doesn't have one in hers. I guess _____ .
    a. he squeaking wheel gets the oil
    b. he who hesitates is lost
    c. forewarned is forearmed

II. Fill in the blanks with proverbs from the list below. Make any necessary changes in capitalization
    and punctuation.

    the first step is always the hardest
    forewarned is forewarmed
    he who hesitates is lost
    if at first you don't succeed, try, try again
    necessity is the mother of invention
    no pain, no gain
    nothing ventured, nothing gained
    the pen is mightier than the sword
    practice makes perfect
    Rome wasn't built in a day
    the squeaking wheel gets the oil
    you're never too old to learn

1. Mountain climbing at age 74?! Well, I guess _____ .

2. Craig takes fifty shots at the basket every day. It's not surprising that he does so well in the big games. _____ .

3. Sam is on a new exercise program to lose weight. He has to run up and down stairs for an hour every day. Sam says, " _____ ."

4. This is a great deal on this car. These prices won't last forever. Buy now! _____ .

5. Fern wants me to join her businesswomen's breakfast club. I don't like to get up early in the morning, but I need to make some good business contacts. I guess I will join. _____ .

6. Sharon was nervous about learning to read. Thelma told her that once she started with Project Read, it all would get easier. _____ .

7. Huang has been working on his garden for months. I asked him why it was taking so long and he said, " _____ ."

8. I'm sorry you failed your driver's license test. You need to study harder next time. _____ .

9. Konstantin forgot his hammer when he went camping, so he used an old tree stump to pound in his tent pegs. _____ .

10. Flo always gets waited on in stores because she makes a big fuss if there aren't any clerks around. It's true that _____ .

11. Don't get violent with him. Send a letter to his supervisor. _____ .

12. Before you go to baby-sit for the Averys, let me tell you about baby Gretchen. _____ .

III. Complete the crossword puzzle using the clues below.

Across

1. the _____ is always the hardest

2. the squeaking wheel gets the _____

5. he who _____ is lost

7. nothing _____, nothing gained

9. if at first you don't succeed, _____ again

10. you're never _____ to learn

11. the _____ is mightier than the sword

Down

1. forewarned is _____

2. no pain, no _____

4. Rome wasn't built _____

6. necessity is the mother of _____

8. _____ makes perfect

Answer Key

I. 1. b.   5. a.   9. c.
    2. a.   6. b.   10. b.
    3. a.   7. c.   11. c.
    4. c.   8. b.   12. a.

II. 1. you're never too old to learn   7. Rome wasn't built in a day

    2. Practice makes perfect   8. If at first you don't succeed, try, try again

    3. No pain, no gain   9. Necessity is the mother of invention

    4. He who hesitates is lost   10. the squeaking wheel gets the oil

    5. Nothing ventured, nothing gained   11. The pen is mightier than the sword.

    6. The first step is always the hardest   12. Forewarned is forearmed.

III.

	¹F	I	R	S	T	S	T	E	P			
	O											
	R			²G			³O	⁴I	L	
⁵H	E	S	⁶I	T	A	T	E	S		N
	A		N		I					A
	R		⁷V	E	N	T	U	R	E	D
	M		E							A
	E		N			⁹P			Y
	D		⁹T	R	Y	T	R	Y
			I			A
¹⁰T	O	O	O	L	D	C
			N			T
						I
						C
				¹¹P	E	N

Section Five

It Never Works

47.   Beggars Can't Be Choosers

Look before You Leap

Ask the class the following questions:

How is the man on the left dressed? What do his clothes tell you about him? Describe his appearance. Why do you suppose he is carrying his hat upside down? What does he seem to be doing with his left hand? How about the man with the glasses? How is he dressed? What do his clothes indicate about him? What is he doing with his left hand? How do you think he feels about the man holding the hat?

Make Hay While the Sun Shines

Ask the class the following questions:

Do you think that a beggar is basically someone who is lazy and refuses to work? Explain your answer. Can you comment on any reasons that would reduce a person to begging? Do you think that persons receiving welfare are practicing some form of begging? Comment on the difference between a street beggar and someone who receives aid from a welfare agency. Do you believe the only people receiving financial aid are those that have no incentive to seek employment? Explain your answer. Can you think of social or economic conditions that might cause financial hardship in a family? In your native country are there many beggars? How are they generally treated by those who are more fortunate? Do financial aid or welfare programs exist in your native country? If so, in which ways do they help the needy? If not, how do the needy survive? Have you ever been in a position of need? What were the circumstances? Was the need temporary or long-lasting? How was it resolved? Do you think that a person in need is thankful to receive that which is offered? Could that person also be resentful of the small amount of the offer? Have you ever given money to someone in need? If so, what prompted you to do so? If not, why not?

A Friend Who Shares . . .

Present this situation to the students for discussion:

Kirk, a student with limited funds, decided to buy a nice box of candy for his girlfriend for Valentine's Day. A big, red box in the shape of a heart caught his eye. He wanted to purchase it, but it turned out to be too expensive, so he had to settle for something smaller and more ordinary in appearance. What thought ran through his mind as he was paying for the candy?

Nothing Ventured, Nothing Gained

Have the students compose (orally or in writing) a speech or monologue based on the following situation:

When Cheryl heard that one of her favorite concert artists was coming to town for a special one-night performance she was elated and went out to get a ticket for the concert. Much to her chagrin all the good tickets had already been sold out. The only tickets available were those in the upper balcony, far from the stage. She ended up buying a ticket for a less desirable seat since she felt that she had no choice if she wanted to attend the concert at all.

48.   Clothes Do Not Make the Man

Look before You Leap

Ask the class the following questions:

What is the man wearing? Can you describe his outfit? What is it called? Do people ordinarily dress in this manner? Why do you suppose he is dressed like that? In past times who used to wear outfits like the one depicted in the illustration? Why? How do you suppose a person would feel dressed in this manner? Explain.

Make Hay While the Sun Shines

Ask the class the following questions:

Can you name other articles of clothing? Which are worn by men and which by women? Which are worn in warm weather? Which in cold weather? Can you comment on how clothing styles have changed through the years? Include both men's and women's wear. Do you think it is possible to tell a lot about a person from the way he or she dresses? Why or why not? Can you contrast the type of clothing that is worn for ordinary occasions with the type that is worn on special occasions? Have you ever formed an opinion about a person based on the way he or she is dressed? Describe the occasion. Was your opinion justified? Why? Why not? Do you think that appearances are deceiving? Explain. Do you think that clothes have any kind of effect on a person's behavior or character? If so, under what circumstances? If not, why not? In your opinion is it wrong to judge a person by the way he or she is dressed? What might be the consequences of doing so?

A Friend Who Shares...

Present this situation to the students for discussion:

When a shabbily dressed man entered one of the more elegant restaurants and ordered an expensive meal the waiter wondered what he was doing there and strongly doubted that he would be able to pay for his meal. Not only did the man pay in full for his meal, but he left a hefty tip in the bargain! What do you suppose the waiter was thinking as his customer was leaving the premises?

Nothing Ventured, Nothing Gained

Have the students compose (orally or in writing) a dialogue based on the following situation:

Mr. Spencer, a loan officer in a bank, was sitting at his desk when a distinguished-looking, well-dressed man approached him to negotiate a rather substantial loan. Mr. Spencer greeted him cordially. After making some general inquiries about the customer's financial portfolio, Mr. Spencer felt certain that there would be no problem in granting him the loan. Just as they were about to complete the final paperwork, two plainclothes police officers walked in and arrested the loan applicant for fraud.

49. A Leopard Cannot Change His Spots

Look before You Leap

Ask the class the following questions:

Where is the leopard standing? What does he have in his paw? What is he trying to do? Why? Does it appear that he will be able to accomplish his purpose? Comment on the situation. In what ways do animals usually clean themselves? Do you think that another leopard would find him more appealing if he had no markings on his coat? Comment on the absurdity of the situation.

Make Hay While the Sun Shines

Ask the class the following questions:

The leopard is a member of the cat family. Can you name other members of this family? Can you describe their natural habitats? Do you know if certain members of this family are dangerous and would attack a human being? Explain. Can you describe some of these animals? What do they have in common? In which ways might they differ from one another? How can cats be used by man? Can they be tamed? For what purpose? Do you believe it is possible for a person to change his character? If so, under what circumstances? If not, why not? Can you think of any reasons why a person would want to change? In your opinion is behavior modification lasting? Explain why you think as you do. Have you ever wanted to be like someone else? Why? Was it because you admired the person or was it for other reasons? Have you ever tried to emulate someone else? Were you satisfied with the change in your basic behavior and character? Did you find that you were more accepted by others as a result? Describe your experience. Do you accept people as they are, or do you try to change others? Are your efforts successful? Describe the situation and the outcome.

A Friend Who Shares . . .

Present this situation to the students for discussion:

Craig, an inveterate gambler, approached his aunt for a loan. Craig told her he had been having some financial problems and needed the money for food and other living expenses. His aunt refused to lend him the money. What thought occurred to her when Craig approached her for the loan?

Nothing Ventured, Nothing Gained

Have the students compose (orally or in writing) a speech or monologue based on the following situation:

A certain neighborhood was up in arms over a series of robberies that had been taking place lately. The police finally apprehended the robber and recognized him as a man who had recently been released from prison for the same offense. Naturally, no one was surprised.

50. Man Does Not Live by Bread Alone

Look before You Leap

Ask the class the following questions:

Does it appear that the man and woman depicted in the illustration know each other? What is the reason for your opinion? What is the man carrying? Where might he have been going? Why do you suppose he turned his head? How about the woman? Where might she have been going? Does it seem that she is interested in the man? Explain.

Make Hay While the Sun Shines

Ask the class the following questions:

Bread is said to be the "staff of life." What does this expression mean? Do you know the ingredients that go into the making of bread? What types of bread can you name? From what flour are they made? Is bread a pastry? What do the two have in common? How are they different? Can you name other pastry? Do you believe that a person can sustain himself on bread and water alone? Explain why or why not. Besides food, can you name some other basic human needs? What can be the effects of being deprived of these needs? Is the harm only physical or can it also be psychological? In what ways? Describe both aspects of the question. Can you describe some of your own personal needs? Which of them do you consider basic to your well-being? Which can be of a lesser priority?

A Friend Who Shares . . .

Present this situation to the students for discussion:

While visiting his friend, Jerrad, Marcus congratulated him on the purchase of his compact disc player. Jerrad told his friend how pleased he was with his acquisition but admitted that he was feeling a bit guilty because the money he spent on the disc player really should have gone for his weekly living expenses. Marcus, knowing that the disc player would provide many hours of happy listening for his friend, patted him on the back and alleviated Jerrad's guilt. What do you suppose Marcus said to him?

Nothing Ventured, Nothing Gained

Have the students compose (orally or in writing) a dialogue based on the following situation:

While taking his afternoon stroll through the park, Mr. Carson came upon his next-door neighbor, Hillary. She was seated on one of the benches and was deeply engrossed in a novel. Hillary explained to Mr. Carson that although she needed money, she decided to take a day off from work because she needed the rest and relaxation more.

51. Money Does Not Grow on Trees

Look before You Leap

Ask the class the following questions:

What is the tree doing? What is it attempting to show? How is the tree trying to prove that there is nothing in its pockets? Judging from his clothes, what can you deduce about the man on the right? Why do you suppose he is holding his hat in his hand? What does he want? Why? Does it appear that the man will get what he's after? Explain. Why do you suppose the man approached the tree in the first place?

Make Hay While the Sun Shines

Ask the class the following questions:

Can you name the parts of a tree? What names of trees do you know? What types of trees grow in your native country? Are they like the trees you have seen in the United States? Explain. In what ways do trees serve the needs of humans? Can you name any products that come from trees? Do you know what substance comes from the bark of certain trees? Can you make any association with money and trees? Why do people say that money does not grow on trees? Consider the color of money and the color of the leaves of a tree. Comment on your impression. If a person needs money, what sources can he or she explore? In most cases people have to work for their money. Can you think of people who do not have to do so? How do these people come by their money? Would you say that they come into their money by honest means? Do you believe that money brings happiness? Discuss your feelings.

A Friend Who Shares...

Present this situation to the students for discussion:

Stanley was invited by friends to go on a weekend ski trip. However, he was somewhat short on cash and asked his father to advance him some money. His father had just finished paying the monthly bills and was feeling a financial pinch. In view of the fact that money was tight, what do you imagine he said to his son when Stanley asked him for money for his trip?

Nothing Ventured, Nothing Gained

Have the students compose (orally or in writing) a dialogue based on the following situation:

Mr. Swensen loved to build things. On weekends he could be heard sawing and pounding away in his garage. One day, when he came home with an expensive new set of tools, his wife hit the ceiling. Mrs. Swensen had been saving every penny she could to buy shoes for the children, and now her husband had exceeded the limits of their budget by splurging on a set of tools! She reproached him for his foolhardiness and reminded him that money was in short supply.

52.   One Swallow Does Not a Summer Make

Look before You Leap

Ask the class the following questions:

What is the bird wearing? Why? What is the season of the year? How can you tell? Where is the bird perched? What reason would it have for being there all alone? Is it trying to tell us something? Does it appear that the bird could be lost? Where do you suppose the rest of the flock might be located? Does the bird look unhappy? If not, what reason could it have for being there? Do you think that it might have departed from the flock in search of food? Explain.

Make Hay While the Sun Shines

Ask the class the following questions:

What kinds of birds can you name? In what regions are their natural habitats? What are migrating birds? Why do they migrate? Do you know of any birds that can survive in cold climates? Do you think that these birds would survive if they were removed from their natural habitats? Tell why they might or might not. Do you think it is possible to predict how an event will turn out by observing its beginning stages? Explain your reaction. What, in your opinion, would it take to determine with accuracy the final outcome of an event? Have you ever been impressed by someone or something at first glance? Discuss the situation and comment on what it was that drew your admiration. As time passed did you have reason to maintain your enthusiasm? If so, why? If not, why not? What would someone have to do to prove that he or she was a true friend? Would you base a friendship on a single incidence of loyalty? Explain why you feel as you do.

A Friend Who Shares...

Present this situation to the students for discussion:

Garth and Jules were schoolmates. One day Garth, beaming from ear to ear, told his friend that he had just scored 100 percent on his first geography exam! He went on to say that he felt certain that he would be getting an "A" in the course. What reminder did his friend Jules offer?

Nothing Ventured, Nothing Gained

Have the students compose (orally or in writing) a speech or monologue based on the following situation:

Jill lived in a cold climate where winters were quite severe and the snowfall was heavy. One winter day Jill ran excitedly into the house and exclaimed to her parents that winter was over and that spring had finally arrived—she had just seen a flower coming up in the snow. Her parents, being older and wiser, told their daughter that she should not consider winter over just because she saw a flower.

53.   Too Many Chiefs, Not Enough Indians

Look before You Leap

Ask the class the following questions:

Looking at the illustration, can you describe the outfits that the American Indian chiefs are wearing? What are they doing? How do they appear? Would you say that they are calm or excited? How can you tell? Does it seem that they are all saying the same thing? How about the American Indian standing in front of them? Compare his headgear with that of the others. Do you think that the single feather has any significance? Judging from the expression on his face, how would you say he is feeling? Explain. What do you think the three other American Indians are trying to tell him?

Make Hay While the Sun Shines

Ask the class the following questions:

Do you happen to know the names of any of the Indian tribes of America? In what type of dwelling did they once live? Can you describe it? Do you know what now-endangered animal was one of their main sources of food? How did they used to hunt? Do you know how they used to send messages over great distances? How was each tribe governed? Can you comment on the role of the women and children of the tribe? Do you think it is better to have final decisions left in the hands of a single person, or do you think it would be better to have power vested in a council or a group of elders? Comment and give reasons for your opinions. In your job or profession do you have to follow the orders of more than one supervisor? If not, comment on the way you perform your duties. If so, comment on how you feel, especially when you are given conflicting orders. Can you imagine what might or might not take place if a lot of administrators have their own ideas on how something should be done in a situation where there are fewer workers than administrators? Comment on the situation.

A Friend Who Shares...

Present this situation to the students for discussion:

Vivian's friends decided to have a surprise party for her to celebrate her sixteenth birthday. They got together and made elaborate plans to have the party. Unfortunately, the plans were never realized, since no one was willing to take the time and effort to set everything up beforehand. What might be the reason that the party did not take place?

Nothing Ventured, Nothing Gained

Have the students compose (orally or in writing) a speech or monologue based on the following situation:

When the school ran short of money for materials for the gifted program, a group of parents offered to put on a fund-raising event to raise the necessary money. During the meeting that was called to organize the event, two committees were formed. One was the planning committee and the other was to be responsible for carrying out the orders of the first. The majority of the parents volunteered for the planning committee and the school never did receive the money it needed for the special program.

54. You Can Lead a Horse to Water, but You Can't Make Him Drink

Look before You Leap

Ask the class the following questions:

Can you name the gear that is on the horse? Why would you say that the horse is waving one of his hoofs? What is he trying to indicate? How is the cowboy dressed? What kind of hat is he wearing? What does he have around his neck? What type of pants is he wearing? What does he have in his hand? What is he trying to do? Why do you suppose the horse is refusing to drink? Might it be because something is wrong with the water? What do you think?

Make Hay While the Sun Shines

Ask the class the following questions:

Can you comment on the role of horses in general? What used to be their primary function? For what other purposes were they used? How were horses of use to farmers? To the military? To the civilian population? In our time what would you say is the main interest in horses? To your knowledge are horses now being used in other lands as they were in times gone by? Have you ever tried to coax a person into doing something that he did not want to do? What was the situation? Comment on the outcome. Do you think that once a person makes up his or her mind to pursue a certain course of action it is possible to dissuade him or her from following through? State why or why not. Comment on both aspects of the question. Has anybody ever tried to make you do something you did not want to do? How did you react? Was this person eventually successful in convincing you? Do you believe that at times we cannot see ourselves as others see us? Comment. Do you believe that if a person proposes that you modify your behavior, that person might have a valid reason for doing so? Comment. Why do you think that a person might resist following the recommendation of a well-meaning relative or friend?

A Friend Who Shares...

Present this situation to the students for discussion:

This is the third time that Fred has had to attend traffic school because of his tickets for speeding. Apparently, he has not learned that speed can kill. The officer in charge of the session has repeatedly tried to make Fred understand the importance of driving within legal speed limits, but to no avail. What must the officer be thinking each time he sees Fred?

Nothing Ventured, Nothing Gained

Have the students compose (orally or in writing) a speech or monologue based on the following situation:

Professor Higgins has been teaching for many years. During the course of his classroom experience he has encountered all types of students and has found that those who were serious about their studies applied themselves and learned. On the other hand many students had shown little or no interest in his courses. In spite of the fact that he had offered to tutor them personally on a one-to-one basis, they ended up by either dropping or failing the course.

55.   You Can't Have Your Cake and Eat It, Too

Look before You Leap

Ask the class the following questions:

Can you describe the man sitting at the table? What does he have in his hand? What is on the table in front of him? What is he thinking of? Why do you think that there is so little food on his plate? What does this illustration tell you about his eating habits? From all appearances do you believe that he will be able to adhere to a strict dietary regime? State the reasons for your opinion.

Make Hay While the Sun Shines

Ask the class the following questions:

The fork is an implement for eating. What other implements are used at the table? What functions do they perform? Do you know for what reasons people diet? Is it always because they want to lose weight? In your opinion is it hard to stay on a diet? Why? Is a diet the only way to lose weight? Can you name other ways of taking off weight? Do you think that obesity comes about only because a person overeats? What other factors can contribute to obesity? Can you name some foods that are fattening? Do you think that being overweight can be hazardous to your health? How? Have you ever wanted something that you could not have? Describe the situation. Have you ever witnessed a situation where a person did something that he wanted to do and thus caused trouble for someone close to him? If so, outline the situation and state how his or her actions affected the other person. Would you ever do something for personal satisfaction if you felt that what you did would distress someone else?

Explain under what circumstances you might and under what circumstances you would not. Do you think that it is possible to enjoy the advantages of two conflicting situations at the same time? Explain how this might be possible.

A Friend Who Shares... Present this situation to the students for discussion:

Rebecca and Darin wanted to have a big wedding and then go to Hawaii for their honeymoon. Unfortunately, it turned out that they would not have enough money to do both. After some vacillation they decided on the big wedding and settled for a shorter trip to a nearby resort area for their honeymoon. What did they both realize when they were obliged to change their plans?

Nothing Ventured, Nothing Gained Have the students compose (orally or in writing) a dialogue based on the following situation:

Mr. and Mrs. Guardado were in a dilemma over the family vacation. They had wanted to take the kids to Disneyland and then drive down to visit the San Diego Zoo. However, because of the fact that Mr. Guardado was to have only a short vacation, they realized that they would not have enough time to do everything. They decided to eliminate the excursion to San Diego and to concentrate on having a good time in Disneyland.

56. You Can't Teach an Old Dog New Tricks

Look before You Leap Ask the class the following questions:

Can you identify the woman in the picture? What is she wearing around her neck? What type of jacket and pants does she have on? What is she wearing on her feet? What does she have in her hand? What do you think she is trying to do? Is she successful? How would you say she is feeling? What would you say about the dog? Does it appear that it is in a cooperative mood? If not, why not? How might it be feeling?

Make Hay While the Sun Shines Ask the class the following questions:

Have you ever been to a circus? Can you name some of the acts in a circus? What do we call a person who teaches animals to do tricks? Can you name some of the tricks that animals do at the circus? Can you name some of the animals that take part in the acts? Are any of them dangerous? Do you think it is difficult to train an animal? Why or why not? Do you think that some animals are harder to train than others? Why? Do you believe it is possible to learn at any age? Why or why not? Compare the learning ability of young people with that of the elderly. Who learns faster? Why? Do you think it is possible for an elderly person to acquire new skills? How about behavior? Do you think that it is always possible to modify behavior once it has become habit? Do you think that age has anything to do with change? Explain your opinion. Do you know of anybody who has tried to pick up a new skill at an advanced age? Was this person successful? Do you believe that once a person reaches a certain age he or she should not try to modify behavior or learn something new? Comment on these ideas.

A Friend Who Shares...   Present this situation to the students for discussion:

Donald and Charlotte had a good marriage, although Donald was quite a bit older than his wife. They both liked to go dancing and both felt at home with traditional dances. Charlotte, however, also liked the latest, modern styles of dancing. Unfortunately, she could never get her husband to attempt to learn the new dances. What might she be thinking when her husband showed no interest in the more unstructured style of dancing?

Nothing Ventured, Nothing Gained   Have the students compose (orally or in writing) a speech or monologue based on the following situation:

Mrs. Stevens had been teaching elementary school for twenty-five years. She had become set in her ways. One day the principal approached her and asked her to incorporate a new method of teaching language to her first and second graders. Mrs. Stevens had to decline, saying that she was not up on the latest developments in elementary education. She went on to say that she preferred to stay with the old, tried and true methods and techniques.

Practice Makes Perfect

I. Select the best proverb to complete each paragraph.

1. Felicia sold her first story to *True Romances*. Now she says that she will be a professional writer.

    I warned her that _____ .
    a. money doesn't grow on trees
    b. beggars can't be choosers
    c. one swallow does not a summer make

2. Mr. Shih dresses elegantly, but his table manners are terrible. I guess _____ .
    a. you can't have your cake and eat it too
    b. clothes do not make the man
    c. man does not live by bread alone

3. I quit my job as a stockbroker to come out here to Wyoming and herd sheep. I don't make as

    much money as I did before, but _____ .
    a. man does not live by bread alone
    b. money doesn't grow on trees
    c. you can lead a horse to water, but you can't make him drink

4. Gabby presented her landfill proposal to the city council last night. They all said it made sense,

    but they voted against it anyway. _____ .
    a. You can't have your cake and eat it too.
    b. You can lead a horse to water, but you can't make him drink.
    c. Beggars can't be choosers.

5. Val wants the security of marriage, but he won't make a serious commitment to one person. I

    told him _____ .
    a. too many chiefs, not enough Indians
    b. one swallow does not a summer make
    c. you can't have your cake and eat it too

6. Zhou promised to stop spending so much time at the video arcade, but he was there again all day

    yesterday. _____ .
    a. Clothes do not make the man.
    b. A leopard cannot change his spots.
    c. Money does not grow on trees.

7. Vlad wants another new pair of tennis shoes. We just bought him those PowerGlides last week.

    I told him that _____ .
    a. you can't teach an old dog new tricks
    b. money does not grow on trees
    c. a leopard cannot change his spots

8. Our committee meeting lasted for hours and we never came to a decision on anything. We all

   had our own ideas about how to do things. Our problem was _____ .
   a. too many chiefs, not enough Indians
   b. man does not live by bread alone
   c. you can't have your cake and eat it too

9. Just try to convince the school board that this new way to teach algebra is a good idea. Most of the board members have been on the board for years. They won't agree to it.

   _____ .
   a. You can't teach an old dog new tricks.
   b. Clothes do not make the man.
   c. Money does not grow on trees.

10. Floyd took a job sweeping cages at the zoo. It wasn't what he wanted to do, but he couldn't find

    work as an electrician. _____ .
    a. A leopard cannot change his spots.
    b. One swallow does not a summer make.
    c. Beggars can't be choosers.

II. Complete the sentences in the following dialogues with proverbs from the list below.

    beggars can't be choosers
    clothes do not make the man
    a leopard cannot change his spots
    man does not live by bread alone
    money does not grow on trees
    one swallow does not a summer make
    too many chiefs, not enough Indians
    you can lead a horse to water, but you can't make him drink
    you can't have your cake and eat it too
    you can't teach an old dog new tricks

Dialogue 1

    Pat: How was your job interview yesterday?

    Fran: Okay. But I wasn't exactly excited about the corporation.

           _____ .
           (Too many people are giving orders, and not enough people are following orders)

    Pat: Maybe it's not that way all the time. _____
                                                (One piece of evidence is not enough to prove

           _____ .
           something)

Fran: True, but everyone there dressed like a CEO.

Pat: Well, _____ .
            (a person should not be judged by the clothes he or she wears)

Fran: You're right. Besides, they offered me the job and I really need a job right now.
_____ .
            (When a person has nothing, he or she must accept whatever help is offered.)

Dialogue 2

Carlos: It's so hot in Old Samuel's room. Won't he buy a fan?

Ray: No. You know what he says. _____ .
                                        (Money is not easily obtained.)

Carlos: But fans are cheap.

Ray: I know that, but Old Samuel has never owned a fan and _____
                                                                    (elderly people can't

_____ .

            change their behavior or learn anything new)

Carlos: Maybe you could persuade him.

Ray: Not likely. _____
                        (You can propose a course of action to someone, but you can't force that

_____ .

            person to accept it.)

Carlos: Old Samuel has never liked "modern conveniences." _____ .
                                                                (A person cannot change his or her

_____ .

            basic character once it has been formed.)

Dialogue 3

Ho: I'm going to be a forest guide.

Hui: You won't make much money at that.

Ho: True, but I'll be outside in the mountains and forest. _____
                                                            (People's psychological needs as

_____ .

            well as their physical needs must be satisfied if they are to live.)

Hui: That makes sense to me, but what about your accounting clients?

Ho: I'll keep them. That way I'll still have a good income.

Hui: _____ .
(You can't enjoy the advantages of two conflicting activities at once.)

III. Unscramble the following proverbs.

1. choosers / be / beggars / can't

_____

2. many / enough / , / not / chiefs / too / Indians

_____

3. by / not / alone / man / live / does / bread

_____

4. old / new / tricks / you / teach / an / dog / can't

_____

5. lead / can't / him / water / you / but / a / , /
   can / drink / to / make / horse / you

_____

_____

6. make / one / summer / does / swallow / not / a

_____

7. man / make / not / the / clothes / do

_____

8. trees / on / money / not / grow / does

_____

9. eat / cake / have / too / and / it / you / can't / your

_____

10. cannot / his / change / spots / a / leopard

_____

Answer Key

I.   1. c.   5. c.   9. a.
       2. b.   6. b.   10. c.
       3. a.   7. b.
       4. b.   8. a.

II. **Dialogue 1**
Too many chiefs, not enough Indians.
One swallow does not a summer make.
clothes do not make the man.
Beggars can't be choosers.

Dialogue 2
Money does not grow on trees.
you can't teach an old dog new tricks.
You can lead a horse to water, but you can't make him drink.
A leopard cannot change his spots.

Dialogue 3
Man does not live by bread alone.
You can't have your cake and eat it too.

III. 1. beggars can't be choosers
     2. too many chiefs, not enough Indians
     3. man does not live by bread alone
     4. you can't teach an old dog new tricks
     5. you can lead a horse to water, but you can't make him drink
     6. one swallow does not a summer make
     7. clothes do not make the man
     8. money does not grow on trees
     9. you can't have your cake and eat it too
   10. a leopard cannot change his spots

Section Six
It's Human Nature

57.   The Apple Does Not Fall Far from the Tree

Look before You Leap

Ask the class the following questions:

What does the man have around his head? What does he have around his waist? What type of garment is he wearing? Can you describe the position of his right arm? How about his left arm? In what position are his eyes? In what sport is he preparing to engage? How about the boy? Can you compare him to the man? Do you think the two might be related? Why?

Make Hay While the Sun Shines

Ask the class the following questions:

What kind of sport is judo? Do you know where it originated? Can you describe how it is practiced? Is it similar to the American sport of boxing? Can you compare the two? Are the feet used more in one than in the other? How? Can you think of another sport that is similar to judo? Why might a person be interested in learning judo? Can you describe different ways in which people can protect themselves from physical harm from someone? Do you have someone whom you admire a great deal? Why? Describe the person. Is it a friend or a relative? As you were growing up, did you have any ambitions or desires to take up a certain profession as an adult? If so, what profession? What was the source of your inspiration? Were you self-motivated, or did you imitate someone else? What do you think of your father's profession? Is it something that you would want to do as an adult? Comment on why or why not. Do you believe that a child's parents can influence his or her choice of friends? What about his choice of profession? Examine the aspects of each question and state reasons for your answers. In which ways do children take after their parents? Consider and comment on language and cultural heritage.

A Friend Who Shares . . .

Present this situation to the students for discussion:

Judd, a football coach, was on the point of retiring. Nevertheless, he felt that he would still be involved in football vicariously through his son, Curtis, who had just been hired as a quarterback on one of the NFL teams. What do you suppose that people would say about Curtis when they became aware of the fact that he would be playing professional football?

Nothing Ventured, Nothing Gained

Have the students compose (orally or in writing) a speech or monologue based on the following situation:

Ever since Donna could remember, her mother had been involved in dance. As a little girl Donna did not show much interest in taking dance at her mother's studio. However, one day, when she saw a performance by a renowned ballet dancer, she was smitten and decided to pursue a career in dance. Eventually, Donna became a well-known choreographer.

58.   Barking Dogs Seldom Bite

Look before You Leap

Ask the class the following questions:

What is the size of the dog in the illustration? From what you see, would you say that the dog has a small bark? Is it intimidating? Explain. Does it appear that the dog could make someone afraid of it? Why or why not? Do you think that it could really hurt someone? Explain. How about the man? Contrast his size with that of the dog. Why do you suppose the dog is barking at him? Does it appear that the man is frightened of the dog? Why not? Does he think the dog will hurt him? Explain why you believe as you do.

Make Hay While the Sun Shines

Ask the class the following questions:

The dog is a member of the canine family. Can you name other members of this family? Are any of these members domesticated? Which ones might be used as pets? Why or why not? Can you name some breeds of dogs? Can you describe them? People say that dogs are man's best friend. Do you agree? Explain the reasons for your opinion. Do you usually get frightened when a dog barks at you? Why or why not? Does the fact that a dog barks mean that it is on the verge of attacking? Explain. For what reasons do dogs bark? Have you ever been threatened by anybody? What were the circumstances? Did the person or thing that threatened you actually follow through? Did you feel intimidated to the point that you had to submit so as not to be hurt? Explain. What was the final outcome? Were you actually hurt in some way? Do you believe that a person who threatens another person actually means to cause harm if his or her wishes are not complied with? Comment. Why does one person threaten another in the first place?

A Friend Who Shares...

Present this situation to the students for discussion:

Emily was nervous about taking a dress back to a store because the store manager had a reputation for intimidating the customers. However, when the manager saw that the dress had a defect, she gave Emily no trouble with the return. Naturally, Emily was relieved. Knowing the reputation of the manager, and feeling unscathed by the incident, what probably ran through Emily's mind?

Nothing Ventured, Nothing Gained

Have the students compose (orally or in writing) a dialogue based on the following situation:

Hercules was a big boy who had a reputation for throwing his weight around to get what he wanted, especially from people smaller than himself. Although he had never really hurt anyone, his yelling was enough to intimidate most people. One day he terrorized a smaller boy because the boy had refused to lend him a video game. The smaller boy did not give in but ran away. When he related the incident to his classmates, they told him that he had no cause to fear Hercules, since he never used physical force to back up his threats.

59. Better a Live Coward Than a Dead Hero

Look before You Leap

Ask the class the following questions:

Describe the situation of the man in the illustration. Why can't he get away? What do you think will happen to him? What is he doing with his right hand? Why? Who is the other man? What does he have in his left hand? What type of uniform does he have on? What does this tell you about him? What do you think he is getting ready to do? Who is the person hiding behind the wall? What do you suppose she is doing there? Would you say that she is in any imminent danger?

Make Hay While the Sun Shines

Ask the class the following questions:

Can you give the definition of *hero?* Can you name situations where a person might distinguish himself or herself by a heroic act? In your opinion, what are some of the character traits of a hero? Which ones would be the strongest? Do you think that a person who commits a heroic act does so completely without fear? Explain your opinion. Can you think of reasons to admire people other than reasons of extreme courage in a life-threatening situation? What is a coward? Do you think a person is necessarily a coward if he or she flees from a situation that would undoubtedly bring him or her physical harm? Explain why or why not. Have you or anyone you know ever been in a life-threatening situation? Can you describe the incident? How did it turn out? Were any other people involved? What did they do? Did you try to help them? Were you successful? Do you think that a person first thinks of his or her own safety when faced with a situation that involves danger to a loved one? Explain your opinion. What would you think of a person who told you that she fled from a situation in which she could well lose her life so that she could fight again another day? Would you accept her reason as being valid, or would you think her a coward? Explain.

A Friend Who Shares... Present this situation to the students for discussion:

A boxer who had knocked out all of his contenders challenged a young rookie to a bout. The rookie declined. He knew perfectly well that he was not ready to take on the pro. What would the rookie have been thinking of when he refused to fight?

Nothing Ventured, Nothing Gained Have the students compose (orally or in writing) a speech or monologue based on the following situation:

Jack had just been hired as a fire fighter. During a recent fire the fire marshal wanted Jack to check inside the house for people who might possibly be trapped and unable to get out. When Jack approached the house and felt the intense heat from the raging fire, he thought it best not to enter, for surely anyone in the house would be dead by now.

60.   A Fool and His Money Are Soon Parted

Look before You Leap Ask the class the following questions:

What is the man on the left doing? Why? Judging from the expression on his face, would you say that he is enthusiastic about making the purchase? How can you tell? How about the guy on the right? Can you describe him? What does he have in his mouth? Judging from the look on his face, what type of person would you say he is? Does he look like someone you would trust? What is he leaning on? Describe its condition. Would you believe the sign in the window? Why or why not? What would you say about the man who seems ready to buy the car? Why?

Make Hay While the Sun Shines Ask the class the following questions:

Can you name any of the interior and exterior parts of a car? What about the parts of the motor? What do we do when we want to start a car? What do we do when we want to stop the car? Can you name different types of cars? Which type would best suit the needs of a family? How about a single young person? How about a person who would use a car simply as basic transportation to and from work? Can you name any technological gadgetry that drivers buy as options for the basic model? Are you the type of person who believes what a salesperson tells you about the merits of a product? Why or why not? How about the printed or stated price of a product? In what instances might you have reason to accept the price as valid, and in what instances would you have reason to believe the price was inflated? Explain. Do you always spend your money on basic necessities for living or do you sometimes buy luxury items or things you could do without? In your opinion is money spent on something not needed money foolishly spent? Why or why not? Has anybody ever taken advantage of you by encouraging you to buy an item of little or no value for an inflated sum of money? Explain the circumstances. What did you do after discovering that you had been deceived? Can you say why many people spend their money on things that will have no lasting value? What do you think of them?

A Friend Who Shares...   Present this situation to the students for discussion:

Manuel, a young business executive, makes good money working for a big corporation. He spends it just as fast as he makes it. He has saved very little and doesn't stop to think that perhaps tomorrow he might be without a job. What might a wiser, more conservative person say about Manuel's spending habits?

Nothing Ventured, Nothing Gained   Have the students compose (orally or in writing) a speech or monologue based on the following situation:

Willy, like many other teenagers, is very much interested in cars and spends all his free time working on his hot rod. He works part-time after school, and whatever money he makes he spends on parts for his car. His parents, needless to say, are constantly after him to start saving money for his education, but Willy turns a deaf ear to their entreaties.

61.   He Who Laughs Last, Laughs Best

Look before You Leap   Ask the class the following questions:

Who is the woman leaving with? Can you describe him? Judging from the look on her face, how would you say she is feeling? How is her escort feeling? Why? Why do you suppose he has his hand over his lips? Is he happy? Is he smiling? Is he laughing? What do you think is going on? How about the taller man? Judging from the look on his face, how would you think he is feeling? Why? What does he have in his hand? What was he going to do with it? Why? What do you imagine the tall man is thinking of the short man?

Make Hay While the Sun Shines   Ask the class the following questions:

Can you think of things that people might laugh at? Can you say, for instance, why a person might laugh at a clown? What makes a clown funny? Can you think of instances where a person might laugh at another person? Have you ever hurt someone's feelings by laughing at him or her? Describe your experience. Do you think that all people find the same things funny? What makes you laugh? Have you ever been disappointed in a particular venture? Describe. Have you ever been in competition with someone else either for another person's affection or for something you wanted to achieve? Describe the situation and the outcome. Do you believe that persistence pays off? Explain. Have you ever been in a situation where someone had a temporary advantage over you, but in the end you were the one who came out on top? Describe the circumstances and eventual outcome. What did you do to gain the upper hand?

A Friend Who Shares...   Present this situation to the students for discussion:

The residents of Cosmopolis all turned out to cheer their football team on to victory. During the last minutes of the game the visiting team was ahead by five points. The fans were disheartened and thought for sure their team was going to lose. With seconds left to play, one of the Cosmopolis players recovered a fumble and ran fifty yards for a winning touchdown just as the last quarter came to an end. The fans were estatic. What might the fans have been thinking when their team won the game at the last minute?

Nothing Ventured, Nothing Gained

Have the students compose (orally or in writing) a dialogue based on the following situation:

While Arnie and Elmer were on a fishing trip, Arnie kept bragging about the number of fish he had been catching and chided his friend for not having been able to keep up with him. Elmer ignored Arnie's remarks and bided his time. All of a sudden he felt a big tug on his line and brought in one of the biggest fish the two had ever seen! Elmer could not restrain his elation as he observed his friend's crestfallen face.

62.   Old Habits Die Hard

Look before You Leap

Ask the class the following questions:

Who do you think the woman is? What do you think she is trying to do? Does it look like she is succeeding? Explain. Do you know why "Smokers Anonymous" was established? What is the main function of the society? Explain. How about the man leaving the premises? What do you think he was doing there? Why do you think he is leaving? Was he serious about following through with his intention when he began partaking in the activities of the society? Can you comment on the fact that a tobacco store is located right next to a meeting place for Smokers Anonymous? Do you see any contradiction? Explain.

Make Hay While the Sun Shines

Ask the class the following questions:

Why do you suppose that there is such a big push to get people to stop smoking? Can you name some of the effects of smoking? Are they all bad? For what reasons do you suppose that people start smoking? Can you imagine why people who smoke might think that smoking helps them in some way? How? Why do you suppose that people persist in smoking when they know that it is hazardous to their health? Can you name other habits—good or bad? Are all habits associated with physical needs or can the mind play a role in the continuance of a bad habit? Explain. Do you have a habit you would like to be rid of? Describe. Is it easy or difficult to break habits? Can you explain why? What would a person have to do to change his or her behavior? Once people have developed certain likes and dislikes, do you think that they would want to modify their behavior? Explain why or why not.

A Friend Who Shares...

Present this situation to the students for discussion:

Yoram had been playing tennis in the evenings after work for years. One day he collapsed on the court. His doctor told him that in the future he would have to avoid all strenuous activities. Yoram, though, did not take him seriously. It was not long before he was out on the courts playing as much as ever. What could be one of the reasons why he went back to the his favorite sport in spite of his doctor's orders to the contrary?

Nothing Ventured, Nothing Gained

Have the students compose (orally or in writing) a dialogue based on the following situation:

Curtis liked to ride his bike with his friends in his neighborhood after school. One day a careless driver ran into him and caused him serious physical harm. While Curtis was in the hospital he resolved never to get on a bike again. Nevertheless, when he finally recovered it was not long before he was out riding his bike again with his school buddies.

63.   One Man's Gravy Is Another Man's Poison

Look before You Leap

Ask the class the following questions:

What is the man on the left doing? What does he have in his hand? What is he eating? Can you describe chili? Does he seem content? Why would you say so? How about the other guy? What's happening to him? Can you describe the expression on his face? What's coming out of his ears? What does this indicate? What do the two men have in common? How would you explain the difference in their reactions?

Make Hay While the Sun Shines

Ask the class the following questions:

What is a spicy food? Can you name other spicy foods? How do some people react to spicy foods? Why? Can such foods cause discomfort? In what ways? In your native country is it common to prepare foods with spices? Can you describe some typical spicy dishes of your country? How are they prepared? Of what ingredients are they made? What type of foods do you prefer? Why? Can you comment on how tastes might differ from one person to another? Can you name certain foods that are popular with the majority of people? Do you have a particular favorite food? Describe it. How about certain foods that you do not eat? Can you say why you do not like them? What role do you think that culture plays in determining diet? Do you think that it is possible to develop a taste for certain foods or drinks? Comment.

A Friend Who Shares . . .

Present this situation to the students for discussion:

Milt opened a business and worked day and night to make it go. So far, he has not been able to make enough from his business for a decent living. His friend, Bruno, works only half as hard. Bruno asks Milt why anyone would want to continue working so hard for such meager profits. What do you imagine Milt said to his friend in response?

Nothing Ventured, Nothing Gained

Have the students compose (orally or in writing) a dialogue based on the following situation:

Drew worked hard all day and liked to relax watching sports on TV after work. His wife, Fran, was not much of a sports fan and preferred watching sitcoms and miniseries. Outside of their different preferences for TV programs, Drew and Fran got along quite well and took pleasure in doing many things together.

64.   The Spirit Is Willing, but the Flesh Is Weak

Look before You Leap

Ask the class the following questions:

What is the man reaching for? Why? What is he feeling? Does it appear that he will be able to restrain himself from satisfying his desire? What makes you think as you do? Who is the person behind him? What does he represent? Explain. How is he in conflict with the man he is holding? Does it appear that he will be able to keep the first man from giving in to temptation? Can you say why or why not?

Make Hay While the Sun Shines

Ask the class the following questions:

What things tempt you? Do you give in to temptation? Why or why not? What do you do to keep from giving in? Have you ever tried to lose weight? Were you successful? If so, was the weight loss permanent? If not, how do you account for the fact that you gained the weight back? Describe the situation. Can you describe how a person might feel about a craving for something he or she should not have? Can you think of things that are easy to give up? Describe them. How about things that are difficult to give up? Why is it hard to give them up? Have you ever wanted to do something, but been unable? What kept you from doing it? Was the cause physical or mental? Describe your experience. What do you think a person feels when he or she gives in to temptation? Do you believe that it becomes easier to resist temptation as one gets older? Explain why or why not.

A Friend Who Shares...

Present this situation to the students for discussion:

Barry has been a smoker for years. He knows it's bad for him and has been successful in stopping for short periods of time. However, whenever confronted by a crisis or any stressful situation, he can't keep from smoking a cigarette to soothe his nerves. What could one say about the fact that no matter how hard he tries to stop, he simply can't?

Nothing Ventured, Nothing Gained

Have the students compose (orally or in writing) a speech or monologue based on the following situation:

In his youth Mr. Riordan was quite a basketball player. Now that he has grown older, he still tries to play and takes great pleasure in trying to show his grandchildren how good he was. Unfortunately, because of his age, he has lost the agility and coordination he had in his youth, and can no longer move around the way he used to.

65.   There Is No Honor among Thieves

Look before You Leap

Ask the class the following questions:

Who might the man on the left be? Can you describe the look on his face? What is he doing? Can you name the game he is playing? What is on the table? For what reason does the man have cards concealed in his clothes? How about the man on the right? How is he like the man with whom he is playing? Does it appear that the two can trust each other? Why or why not?

Make Hay While the Sun Shines

Ask the class the following questions:

Poker is a popular card game in America. Can you name other popular card games? Can you describe how they are played? What are other popular card games in your native country? Can you describe them? Do you think that most card games are played for fun or for profit? Can you name the four card suits? Besides cards, can you name other games that are played for entertainment? How about games that are played for money? Have you ever gambled? If so, did you win or lose money? Can you describe the incident? Do you think that winning money at games of chance is a matter of luck or skill? Explain. Can you describe a trustworthy person? What must he or she be or have done to earn trust? What qualities in a person inspire trust? If you suspected someone of being dishonest, would you cut off any relationship or contact with that person? Tell why or why not. Since both share common character traits, do you think that one dishonest person can have any type of trusting relationship with another? Explain why you feel the way you do.

A Friend Who Shares...

Present this situation to the students for discussion:

An interesting article appeared in the newspaper about a gang of thieves who broke into an electronics store and set off to transport the stolen goods to their private warehouse. When they arrived, they were horrified to discover that their warehouse had been vandalized by a rival gang. What do you suppose that people thought as they read the article about the incident?

Nothing Ventured, Nothing Gained

Have the students compose (orally or in writing) a dialogue based on the following situation:

One day, while Morris and his friend Ned were walking along the street they came upon a new sports car with the keys in the ignition. Morris thought it would be fun to go out on a joyride and coaxed Ned to come along with him. Since neither of them had any money, they decided to rob a convenience store. Morris told Ned to stay in the car with the motor running, as he went in to accomplish the theft. When Morris came running out of the store with the money, he was thunderstruck to see that Ned had driven off with the car.

66. There's More Than One Way to Skin a Cat

Look before You Leap

Ask the class the following questions:

Who is sitting at the table? What is he doing? What book is he studying? Why? Who are traditionally his greatest adversaries? Describe how it is possible to hide or to escape from them. Do you think that one of the parties has any advantage over the other? Why? In what ways? Does it appear that the character depicted in the drawing will eventually achieve his goal? What might that be? Would it be achieved literally or figuratively? Explain.

Make Hay While the Sun Shines

Ask the class the following questions:

Do you have any idea why rodents, especially mice, inspire fear—especially in women? Do you know where they are usually found? In which ways can rodents be harmful to humans? Do you know what mice usually eat? In your opinion, who is more agile—a cat or a mouse? Explain the reasons for your opinion. Do you think that size has anything to do with agility? Explain why or why not. Have you ever been confronted with a situation or problem that you could not resolve? Describe it. When the resolution to a problem escapes you, do you tend to give up? Why or why not? If you have not been able to accomplish a project in your own way, do you believe there is no other way to accomplish it? Comment. Have you ever sought help in accomplishing a project? Explain the circumstances. Do you believe that a person can solve most of his or her problems by being inventive? Why or why not?

A Friend Who Shares...

Present this situation to the students for discussion:

Mr. and Mrs. Stevens were at their wits' end. Lately, their home had been invaded by a hoard of pests. Despite the measures the Stevenses took to get rid of them, all of their efforts came to naught. They figured there had to be another way of solving the problem. Mr. Stevens picked up the phone and called a pest control service. One week after the exterminator paid a visit, the pests were gone! What do you suppose Mr. Stevens said to Mrs. Stevens when they finally solved their problem?

Nothing Ventured, Nothing Gained

Have the students compose (orally or in writing) a speech or monologue based on the following situation:

Mr. Pappas was on his way to an important meeting with one of his business associates when his car broke down. At first he became quite distressed because he thought he might miss the appointment. He looked around and saw a telephone booth on the corner. He called a taxi. He made the meeting on time. It was simple. In fact, he got there with time to spare.

67.   There's No Fool like an Old Fool

Look before You Leap

Ask the class the following questions:

Where is the man sitting? What does he have on his head? Can you describe it? What word is written on it? Do you know what it means? Can you describe the look on his face? How do you suppose he is feeling? How old would you say the man was? Do you think that people of that age are usually in his position? Explain why or why not.

Make Hay While the Sun Shines

Ask the class the following questions:

Do you know how disciplinary action is usually administered in elementary schools? How about middle schools and high schools? For what reasons might a student be asked to stand in the corner by a teacher? Do you think that this is now a widespread practice in the American public school system? Do you think that children are more or less sensitive than adults? Explain why you think as you do. Can you discuss how you think a child would react to criticism? How about an adult? Do you believe that public criticism can be constructive in any form? How do you think most people—young or old—would react to being disciplined before their peers? Do you think that a person can be intimidated into behaving properly? Why? Have you ever done anything foolish? Can you describe the incident? What happened? What was the eventual outcome? In your opinion can a person learn from his or her mistakes? Do you think that once people sees the error of their ways they never again make the same mistake? Comment. Have you ever observed a foolish act committed by an older person? If so, what was your appraisal of the situation? Was it something that you would never have done? Describe the incident and your reactions. In your opinion, when two people of different ages do something foolhardy does one of them seem more ridiculous than the other? Describe an incident, if you know of one, and explain your point of view concerning the question. Do you think that in spite of our best efforts, we do foolish things at any age?

A Friend Who Shares . . .

Present this situation to the students for discussion:

Because you love your father, you often become concerned and even angry over what he does. He's overweight and has a heart problem. The doctor has advised him to keep away from fattening foods and salt. Yet, your father insists on eating greasy foods and heavily salted french fries. In warning him to heed his doctor's advice, what might you tell him?

Nothing Ventured, Nothing Gained

Have the students compose (orally or in writing) a speech or monologue based on the following situation:

Through the years Jean-Philippe has always purchased a certain make of car because he liked its appearance. Nonetheless, the cars manufactured by that company proved to be unreliable and inordinately expensive to repair. Now that it is time for a new car, Jean-Philippe says he won't consider looking at cars from another manufacturer.

68. Variety Is the Spice of Life

Look before You Leap

Ask the class the following questions:

Can you describe the man sitting at the desk? How is he dressed? What does he have on his desk? What would you say that he has been doing? Who might the woman standing in the doorway be? What does she have in her hands? What do you think she is asking the man? Does it appear that he will accept? Explain why or why not. What reason might she have for disturbing his work? Do you think she has her own interests in mind? Explain.

Make Hay While the Sun Shines

Ask the class the following questions:

Can you name different professions that involve a lot of paperwork? What type of papers do teachers have to prepare and correct? How about an office worker? An employee of a department store? A police officer? Can you think of others? How do you feel about your job? Can you describe your duties? Do you find your job interesting? Tedious? Comment on why you feel as you do. Is there much room for advancement? Do you find that you work a lot of overtime? If so, is it because you enjoy your work, or is it because of the money? What other things do you enjoy doing? Do long hours at work keep you from doing them? Explain. At times do you long to get away from your daily routine? Why? What would you like to do? Where might you like to go? Can you name some ways that people relax? In your opinion which is more stressful for a person; physical fatigue or mental fatigue? Explain. What might one do to alleviate mental fatigue? How about physical fatigue? Do you believe that any change in a person's daily routine necessarily has a positive effect? Say why or why not. Illustrate by citing a situation from your own experience.

A Friend Who Shares . . .

Present this situation to the students for discussion:

Although she was a pretty girl, Marlene was a loner and rather antisocial. She followed the same old routine day after day: get up in the morning, go to work, watch TV at night, and then off to bed. One day, when one of her friends suggested that they go out for dinner and a movie, Marlene declined, saying that she was not up to it. It took some doing, but her friend finally convinced Marlene to take her up on her invitation. What do you imagine Marlene's friend told her?

Nothing Ventured, Nothing Gained

Have the students compose (orally or in writing) a speech or monologue based on the following situation:

Felix had been working for years as an accountant. Although he was making good money, he was not happy with his job. One day he decided that it was time for a career change. He went back to college and got a teaching certificate for math. He's now teaching in one of the local high schools and feels that life has opened up for him.

69.   When the Cat's Away the Mice Will Play

Look before You Leap

Ask the class the following questions:

Where is one of the mice? What is he doing? What is the other one doing? Where are they? What is written on the side of the container? What type of a container is it? Does it seem that it is basically used for entertainment? Why do you suppose that the mice are there in the first place? Do you think that they feel safe? Why?

Make Hay While the Sun Shines

Ask the class the following questions:

Can you say why people might try to hide their actions? Do you think they are basically dishonest when they try to do so? Do you think small children bear more watching than, say, teenagers? Explain why or why not. Have you ever had the occasion to do something against your parents' wishes? Can you describe what it was? Why didn't you want them to know? Do you believe that a person will naturally misbehave when no one is watching? What might or might not that person do? In your opinion is "misbehaving" a malicious thing? Why or why not? Do you think that satisfying a desire is necessarily a bad thing to do? Under what circumstances might it not be acceptable? Under what circumstances might it be acceptable? Have you ever done something that you regretted? Did your behavior have an effect on anyone else? Was it a positive or negative effect? Comment. Can you describe a situation where someone has been caught doing something wrong? What was the outcome? Was this person punished or was the incident overlooked? Explain what happened.

A Friend Who Shares...

Present this situation to the students for discussion:

When Kevin's father came home with a brand-new car, Kevin's eyes almost popped out of his head! It was love at first sight. He couldn't wait to drive it. However, his dad told him not to touch the car when he was not at home. In spite of his father's admonition, Kevin used to sneak the car out for a spin in the afternoons before his dad came home from work. When Kevin's friends saw him driving around in his father's car, what do you think they said to him?

Nothing Ventured, Nothing Gained

Have the students compose (orally or in writing) a speech or monologue based on the following situation:

Mrs. Cosper kept a pretty tight lid on her fourth graders when class was in session. Admittedly, it was difficult to do, since the kids were bursting with excess energy. One day, when she was called away from class for a few moments, she came back to find the students running around, and the classroom in total disarray.

Practice Makes Perfect

I. Select the proverb from the list below that best fits each situation.

    a. The apple doesn't fall far from the tree.
    b. Barking dogs seldom bite.
    c. Better a live coward than a dead hero.
    d. A fool and his money are soon parted.
    e. He who laughs last, laughs best.
    f. Old habits die hard.
    g. One man's gravy is another man's poison.
    h. The spirit is willing, but the flesh is weak.
    i. There is no honor among thieves.
    j. There's more than one way to skin a cat.
    k. There's no fool like an old fool.
    l. Variety is the spice of life.
    m. When the cat's away the mice will play.

1. My grandpa bought another used car. The last three used cars he bought all had serious engine problems. _____

2. John wants me to go to another hockey game with him tonight. I like John and John likes hockey. But I really don't enjoy hockey. _____

3. Those tough kids were yelling awful things at me. They were trying to get me to fight with them. I just walked away. _____

4. I'm sorry I left my coffee cup in the living room again. I just can't seem to remember to put it in the kitchen. _____

5. When I'm on vacation, I like to stay in a different place every night. That way, I can see a lot of different things. _____

6. Frank really wants to lose weight, but when he saw that piece of double chocolate cake with cherries, he ate it. _____

7. Look at little Andy. He sits at the computer just like his father. _____

8. Greg has a home full of junk. He stops at every garage sale he sees, and he always buys something. _____

9. When the teacher left the room for a few minutes, the students began throwing paper airplanes out the window. _____

10. If Mr. Zexel won't approve my vacation request, I'll go ask Ms. Martinez. One way or another, I'll get that vacation. _____

11. Bud was bragging about how he copied Sherrie's homework without her knowing it. But Sherrie did know! Yesterday she wrote all the wrong answers on her paper, and Bud copied them.

   _____

12. Don't be upset that Mr. Colomb yelled at you and threatened to fire you. He does that a lot, but he never fires anyone. _____

13. Ty said if I helped him cheat Lara, he would give me half of the money. I helped him, but he didn't give me any of the money. _____

II. Match the proverbs in column A with the example sentences in column B.

	A		**B**
1.	The apple doesn't fall far from the tree.	a.	Dishonest people can't trust each other.
2.	Barking dogs seldom bite.	b.	He's done it that way for years. He won't change.
3.	Better a live coward than a dead hero.	c.	He ran away, but he wasn't hurt.
4.	A fool and his money are soon parted.	d.	She walks just like her mother.
5.	He who laughs last, laughs best.	e.	She keeps believing that man even though he's lied to her for years.
6.	Old habits die hard.	f.	Let's visit every capital in Europe!
7.	One man's gravy is another man's poison.	g.	We don't do any work when the boss is out.
8.	The spirit is willing, but the flesh is weak.	h.	Fran will buy anything that looks antique.
9.	There is no honor among thieves.	i.	Joe laughed at Maria's poetry, but Maria won the school writing award.
10.	There's more than one way to skin a cat.	j.	I didn't mean to eat that piece of pie, but it looked so good.

11. There's no fool like an old fool.

12. Variety is the spice of life.

13. When the cat's away the mice will play.

k. Don't believe her threats.

l. How can you eat squid? I can't even look at it!

m. If I can't win fairly, then I'll cheat.

III. Find and circle the italicized parts of these proverbs. Be sure to look horizontally, vertically, and diagonally.

the apple doesn't fall *far from the tree*
barking dogs seldom bite
better a live coward than *a dead hero*
a fool and his money are soon parted
he who laughs last, *laughs best*
old habits die hard
one man's gravy is another man's poison
the spirit is willing, but *the flesh is weak*
there is no honor among *thieves*
there's more than one way to *skin a cat*
there's no fool like *an old fool*
variety is *the spice of life*
when *the cat's away* the mice will play

a	b	c	y	v	a	r	g	s	n	a	m	e	n	o	p	y	j	w	e	s
f	i	a	m	n	h	b	v	c	x	z	a	s	d	l	f	g	h	k	e	u
o	l	q	r	s	e	w	e	r	t	a	n	o	l	d	f	o	o	l	r	p
o	y	u	i	k	f	o	p	o	a	s	t	b	m	h	o	l	e	r	t	c
l	z	b	x	i	i	n	c	m	v	l	g	k	f	a	j	d	h	s	e	k
a	q	e	w	n	l	n	r	l	a	u	g	h	s	b	e	s	t	e	h	e
n	p	y	o	a	f	t	g	i	r	u	e	y	w	i	t	q	u	o	t	t
d	g	d	o	c	o	f	s	d	k	h	i	r	s	t	o	i	n	h	m	r
h	w	e	r	a	e	n	d	b	o	j	i	u	d	s	s	b	i	v	o	l
i	l	m	e	t	c	p	o	q	a	g	z	z	b	d	a	e	r	d	r	g
s	t	h	h	u	i	r	w	v	x	c	s	c	a	i	v	m	k	t	f	j
m	a	t	d	b	p	d	e	s	a	t	y	i	o	e	m	c	r	s	r	a
o	a	s	a	r	s	e	t	h	e	f	l	e	s	h	i	s	w	e	a	k
n	u	r	e	t	e	m	v	c	k	j	i	p	w	a	z	x	g	d	f	r
e	i	s	d	w	h	a	t	r	e	b	a	b	n	r	k	e	r	v	c	i
y	a	w	a	s	t	a	c	e	h	t	p	o	v	d	e	r	p	t	y	e

Answer Key

I. 1. k.
    2. g.
    3. c.
    4. f.
    5. l.
    6. h.
    7. a.

    8. d.
    9. m.
    10. j.
    11. e.
    12. b.
    13. i.

II. 1. d.
    2. k.
    3. c.
    4. h.
    5. i.
    6. b.
    7. l.

    8. j.
    9. a.
    10. m.
    11. e.
    12. f.
    13. g.

```
a  b  c  y  v  a  r  g  s  n  a  m  e  n  o  p  y  j  w  e  s
f  i  a  m  n  h  b  v  c  x  z  a  s  d  l  f  g  h  k  e  u
o  l  q  r  s  e  w  e  r  t  a  n  o  l  d  f  o  o  l  r  p
o  y  u  i  k  f  o  p  o  a  s  t  b  m  h  o  l  e  r  t  c
l  z  b  x  i  i  n  c  m  v  l  g  k  f  a  j  d  h  s  e  k
a  q  e  w  n  l  n  r  l  a  u  g  h  s  b  e  s  t  e  h  e
n  p  y  o  a  f  t  g  i  r  u  e  y  w  i  t  q  u  o  t  t
d  g  d  o  c  o  f  s  d  k  h  i  r  s  t  o  i  n  h  m  r
h  w  e  r  a  e  n  d  b  o  j  i  u  d  s  s  b  i  v  o  l
i  l  m  e  t  c  p  o  q  a  g  z  z  b  d  a  e  r  d  r  g
s  t  h  h  u  i  r  w  v  x  c  s  c  a  i  v  m  k  t  f  j
m  a  t  d  b  p  d  e  s  a  t  y  i  o  e  m  c  r  s  r  a
o  a  s  a  r  s  e  t  h  e  f  l  e  s  h  i  s  w  e  a  k
n  u  r  e  t  e  m  v  c  k  j  i  p  w  a  z  x  g  d  f  r
e  i  s  d  w  h  a  t  r  e  b  a  b  n  r  k  e  r  v  c  i
y  a  w  a  s  t  a  c  e  h  t  p  o  v  d  e  r  p  t  y  e
```

Section Seven
Friend or Foe?

70. Absence Makes the Heart Grow Fonder

Look before You Leap

Ask the class the following questions:

What is the woman holding in her hands? Who might be the person in her thoughts? How would you say she is feeling toward this person? Can you describe him? What is he holding in one of his hands? What is he doing with his other hand? What does this indicate? How would you imagine he is feeling toward the woman? How does she feel toward him? Can you tell if they have been apart for any length of time? Does it appear that they soon will forget each other? Do you think that their feelings will endure? Explain why or why not.

Make Hay While the Sun Shines

Ask the class the following questions:

Can you name different kinds of pictures? Why do some people carry certain photographs on their person? Of whom are they? Have you ever had occasion to be away from a loved one? What was the occasion? Can you describe your feelings? Did you correspond often? Describe the nature of your correspondence. During your absence what did you do to keep your friend or loved one in mind? Did you miss them more, or did you find someone else to take their place? Explain. Do you believe that love can grow stronger as the years pass? Why or why not? Have you ever had occasion to become disenchanted with a friend or someone who had been close to you? Describe the situation. For what reasons can people grow apart? Do you believe that love is lasting? Does it remain strong for a long period of time or does it eventually fade? In your opinion does a person feel as intensely about another person when he or she is separated from that person for a prolonged period of time? Do you believe that the saying "out of sight, out of mind" is true? Comment on a situation where this might or might not be true.

A Friend Who Shares...

Present this situation to the students for discussion:

Moglie had been the family pet ever since the children were little. Now that they were grown they still were greatly attached to him, although they often took him for granted. When Moglie got sick and had to stay for a week in a pet hospital, everyone began missing him a great deal. Why would you think so?

Nothing Ventured, Nothing Gained

Have the students compose (orally or in writing) a speech or monologue based on the following situation:

Garth and Marsha had been married for only a year when Garth was suddenly called for active duty in the army. They had never been separated before. Of course, Marsha thinks about him night and day and yearns for his return. Now that he's gone, she feels that she loves him more than ever.

71. Beauty Is in the Eye of the Beholder

Look before You Leap

Ask the class the following questions:

What kind of animal do you see in the illustration? Does it look like anything you've ever seen? Can you describe the heads? Why do you suppose one head is looking at the other one? Do you think they find each other attractive? Why or why not? In which direction would the animal go if it were walking or running? Might it have any problems in deciding which way to go? Explain. How do you think that other animals might react to the animal depicted in the illustration? Explain.

Make Hay While the Sun Shines

Ask the class the following questions:

People are known to admire certain animals either for their appearance or prowess. Name some animals that you admire and tell why. Have you ever thought about what attracts you to another person? Is it appearance? Is it personality? Is it something that you both have in common? Comment. Do you know what a "role model" is? Can you say how someone becomes a role model? Is it because of their accomplishments or skill in a certain discipline? Comment and give reasons why someone would want to emulate another person. How would you define or describe "beauty"? Is your definition based entirely on physical appearance? Are there any other factors that contribute to a person's beauty? Do you think there are certain people that are universally considered beautiful? Why? What is there about them so many people find attractive? Comment. Do you know what is meant by the expression "beauty is only skin deep"? Can you explain the fact that some people might consider a man with no hair handsome, or be attracted to someone with a physical shortcoming or imperfection? Discuss. Do you know what is meant by *inner beauty?* Do you think that all people have identical views of what constitutes inner beauty? Discuss your ideas. Can you comment on a situation where you have liked someone or something, but your enthusiasm has not been shared by a friend or associate? How would you define *ugly?* Are there some things that would be universally considered unattractive or repugnant? Can you describe some of them? Do you think that a physical imperfection is ugly? Explain why or why not. Do you think that what may be unattractive to one person may be attractive to another? Comment.

A Friend Who Shares...

Present this situation to the students for discussion:

Your friend, Carl, a lover of art, expresses his admiration for a modern painting he has just seen. He takes you to the museum to look at it and you tell him that you find it bland and unattractive. Since you do not share his opinion, what would you say to him?

Nothing Ventured, Nothing Gained

Have the students compose (orally or in writing) a dialogue based on the following situation:

In preparation for her date with Alvin, Harriet went out and purchased a new dress. She was convinced that she looked very attractive in it and was excited about showing it off for her best friend, Judith. When Judith saw it, she expressed the opinion that the dress was not all that attractive and that it did very little to show off Harriet's figure.

72. Blood Is Thicker Than Water

Look before You Leap

Ask the class the following questions:

Can you describe the family on the left? What do their facial expressions tell you about the way they are feeling? What emotions might they be showing? Does it appear that they all share the same emotion? Explain. How do the two women on the left have their arms? What could this indicate? Can you describe the stance of the little girl? Would you say that she is pleasantly disposed to the little boy on the right? How about the family on the right? Can you contrast their facial expressions with those of the family on the left? How would you say that the individual members of each family feel toward each other? What do both families have in common? What might each family have against the other? Judging from the situation depicted in the illustration, would you say that the two families are having a dispute? Does it appear that they are likely to resolve it? Comment. Would you say that the members of each respective family all share the same views? What makes you think so?

Make Hay While the Sun Shines

Ask the class the following questions:

Anger and love are basic emotions. Can you name others? Are these emotions necessarily confined to humans? Explain. Can you describe the behavior of angry people? How about the behavior of people who are sad or happy? In your opinion, is loyalty an emotion? Explain. Can you comment on what inspires loyalty in a person? Do you think that there are circumstances where one person might be loyal to another, even though that person may not deserve the other's loyalty? Comment. Do you have a friend to whom you feel close? Explain why. Do you always take your friend's side when he or she has a controversy with someone else? Explain why or why not. How about relatives or members of your family? How do you react when one of them is threatened by an outside source? Comment on the reasons for your reaction. Can you describe an incident where you have had to support the cause of a person whom you believed to be in the wrong? Comment. In the course of daily living, how do you react in a controversial situation with one of your parents or with a brother or sister? Can you describe one such incident? How did you behave? Why? What was the final outcome? Was the dispute resolved, or was it left hanging? Explain. Have you ever heard the adage "My country, right or wrong"? Can you say to what it refers? Do you agree with it? Do you think it is possible to feel closer and more loyal to an outsider than to a member of your own family? Explain under what circumstances this might happen.

A Friend Who Shares...

Present this situation to the students for discussion:

Brad was walking along the beach when he heard some cries for help. He looked out at the waves and saw two young boys who were being pulled out by the tide. He recognized one of them as his younger brother and immediately ran out to try to save him. Why do you suppose he dived in to save his brother first?

Nothing Ventured, Nothing Gained

Have the students compose (orally or in writing) a dialogue based on the following situation:

Although Larry and Eugene have seen each other off and on for a number of years, they never really formed a solid friendship. One day when Eugene asked Larry for a loan of a small sum of money, Larry declined, saying that he was strapped for money just then. The next week Larry's brother asked him to lend him some money for a down payment on a car. Larry immediately went to the bank and withdrew the money for him.

73. Familiarity Breeds Contempt

Look before You Leap

Ask the class the following questions:

Who is the man with the towel on his arm? Can you describe what he is doing? How is he behaving toward the man seated at the table? Why do you think he is behaving that way with a stranger? Explain. Who are the man and woman seated at the table? Where do you suppose they are? Judging from the expression on their faces, how would you say they are feeling? Are they satisfied with the service? If you were in that situation would you complain? To whom? What would you say?

Make Hay While the Sun Shines

Ask the class the following questions:

Do you know what the headwaiter in a restaurant is called? What are his duties? Generally speaking how is a table set in a restaurant? What about the decor? How does it contribute to the atmosphere of a restaurant? Can you describe the decor of one of your favorite restaurants? Do you have any close friends? Can you say why you feel close to them? With the passage of time have you noticed any faults in them? Describe. Have you ever had any occasion to criticize or to become upset with someone you know well? Describe the situation and the outcome. Did this person's faults turn you away from him or her? Why or why not? Do you feel that you can express your true feelings more with a person that you know well? If so, aren't you afraid of hurting their feelings? Explain. How would you react if someone close to you criticized you for something? Would you accept the remark as constructive criticism, or would you react angrily to what was said? Explain your position and why you might or might not react angrily. Do you think it is possible to keep certain sides of one's personality hidden from a close friend? Comment on why this might or might not be so.

A Friend Who Shares...

Present this situation to the students for discussion:

When Al saw Rhoda it was love at first sight! After several dates together, when they got to know each other better, Al's strong feelings for Rhoda began to cool, as he noticed certain traits of her personality that were not to his liking. After a while they stopped seeing each other. How can you account for the fact that Al's enthusiasm for Rhoda eventually died out?

Nothing Ventured, Nothing Gained

Have the students compose (orally or in writing) a dialogue based on the following situation:

When Stan got accepted as a student at a major university, he was thrilled. Jules, his roommate at the dorm, was a very likable guy from the Midwest. At first they hit it off quite well, but it was not long before Stan became resentful of his roommate's presence. Jules had a nasty habit of cluttering the room with his dirty socks and underwear. Every night before going to bed Jules would go around munching on crackers or causing some other distraction while Stan was trying to study. Stan's attitude toward Jules cooled considerably as they got to know each other.

74. A Friend in Need Is a Friend Indeed

Look before You Leap

Ask the class the following questions:

What animals are depicted in the illustration? What happened to the animal on the left? Can you describe what it is feeling? How would you say it is feeling toward its companion? What is its companion doing? Why? How do you suppose the animal on the left got into that predicament in the first place? What do you think would have happened if its friend had not happened to come by?

Make Hay While the Sun Shines

Ask the class the following questions:

Can you name some of the animals that people like to hunt? Which ones are especially popular for hunting down? Why would you say so? Can you name some of the implements that hunters use? How are they used? Do you consider hunting a sport? Comment on why or why not. Why do you suppose that certain people engage in hunting? Do hunters always kill their prey? If not, why would they want to keep the animal alive? Can you think of any ways that certain animals benefit humankind? Do you have any close friends that have offered to help you out in a time of need? Can you describe the situation and tell how they helped you? Did you ask for their help, or was it volunteered? How can you account for the fact that a person might offer unsolicited help to another? Do you think that he or she might have thoughts of personal gain when doing so? If not, why would a person offer help? Comment. Have you ever helped out a friend in need? Describe the occasion. Can you describe your feelings in offering to help someone in a difficult plight? How do you suppose the other person felt toward you after having received your aid?

A Friend Who Shares... Present this situation to the students for discussion:

When your friend lost his job and could not afford the rent even for a small apartment, you generously invited him to stay with you until he got back on his feet. He ended up by staying for over six months. Yet you offered him food and shelter during the entire period of time he spent with you without once asking for anything in return or making him feel that he was imposing on you. What do you think he might say about your friendship?

Nothing Ventured, Nothing Gained Have the students compose (orally or in writing) a dialogue based on the following situation:

Giovanni had just gone through a divorce and was acutely depressed. His friend Rodolfo, who had just gone through the same thing only months before, understood very well how his friend felt. He invited Giovanni for dinner and a couple of drinks. The two met and sat talking for hours. After their conversation, Giovanni felt a lot better. As he headed for home he thanked his friend for being a good listener and for his comforting words during this stressful time.

75.   A Friend Who Shares Is a Friend Who Cares

Look before You Leap Ask the class the following questions:

What is one of the girls holding in her hand? What is she trying to do? Do you think that she is trying to give her snack away? Why or why not? Does it appear that the other girl will accept the offer? If so, how can you tell? If not, why not? Why do you suppose that the snack was offered in the first place? Do you think that it was because there was something wrong with it? Explain. What words could you use to describe the girl who is offering her friend what she has? Can you describe how the girls are dressed? Do you think that the way they are dressed has any significance in this scenario? Comment.

Make Hay While the Sun Shines Ask the class the following questions:

Ice cream is a dairy product. What other dairy products can you name? Can you describe how some of them are prepared? Are any of them used in the preparation of other foods? With what other foods may they be eaten? Can you describe a generous person? How can he or she show generosity? How about a selfish person? Can you describe such a person? Can you cite any personal experiences with a selfish or generous person? Describe the occasion and how you felt after having had contact with such a person. Have you ever shared anything with a friend? What motivated you to do so? Did you expect something in return for what you did? Do you think that brothers and sisters like to share their toys? Why or why not? Can you compare sharing among family members with sharing among friends? Are they both done freely? Comment. In your opinion is true friendship based on sharing alone? On what other elements does true friendship depend?

A Friend Who Shares...   Present this situation to the students for discussion:
When Paul saw his roommate, Ryan, sitting at his desk laboriously writing out a book report that was due the next day, he offered to lend him his word processor, so as to facilitate the task of turning in a neat, typed copy. Of course, Ryan welcomed the offer. What do you imagine he thought of Paul's making such a generous offer?

Nothing Ventured, Nothing Gained   Have the students compose (orally or in writing) a dialogue based on the following situation:
During lunchtime Tricia saw her good friend, Jackie, sitting alone on a school yard bench. She looked rather desolate, so Tricia went over and sat down beside her. It soon became clear that Jackie had brought no lunch with her. She told her friend that she had forgotten it at home and that she had no money to buy lunch in the cafeteria. Thereupon, Tricia took out a sandwich from her lunch bag and offered half of it to her friend.

76.   Imitation Is the Sincerest Form of Flattery

Look before You Leap   Ask the class the following questions:
Can you describe the man on the left? What is he wearing on his head? What is he carrying in his hand? Is he wearing an ordinary shirt and shoes? How about the little boy? What is he wearing and what is he carrying? What would you say that the little boy is trying to do? Why? Judging from the expression on the man's face, how would you say he is feeling? Why? What do the man's clothes tell you about him? Who could the man be?

Make Hay While the Sun Shines   Ask the class the following questions:
Can you identify the type of armament that the man is carrying? Do you have any idea as to when such armaments were used? For what purpose? Can you name any other garb that is typical of that period? Have you ever been praised for any of your accomplishments or for your appearance? Describe the occasion. What was it about you that others found praiseworthy? Has anybody ever tried to imitate you in any manner? Why? Were they successful? Describe. Can you describe how you might feel when you see that someone has tried to be like you? What types of people do you think that teenagers are most likely to want to emulate? Can you explain why? How about adults? Do you think they admire the same people as do youngsters? Why or why not? Within the realm of your experience, have you found that praise is always justified or deserved? Can you name any instance where this has not been so? Have you ever had reason to lose respect for someone you admired? Why? Describe the situation. Have you ever let anyone down? If so, describe how it happened and what it was that kept you from being able to follow through.

A Friend Who Shares...   Present this situation to the students for discussion:
Jessica bought a new dress and wore it at a party that one of her friends also

attended. The next week, when Jessica bumped into her friend at a piano recital, she was upset to find that her friend was wearing the same dress that she had worn at the party. However, Jessica soon got over her annoyance when she stopped to think about the matter. What prompted her to change her mind?

Nothing Ventured, Nothing Gained

Have the students compose (orally or in writing) a dialogue based on the following situation:

Ms. Silverstein had been lecturing on an outstanding philosopher of the twentieth century and had been giving her students her views on the philosophy of the master. She had asked the students to write a paper in which they were to express their own interpretation of the ideas pointed out in class. While looking over the papers, Ms. Silverstein was somewhat shocked to read her exact words on the paper of one of her students. She thereupon called the student to her office and chided him for not expressing any original thought. In defending what he had written, the student told his professor that she should be flattered.

77.   Love Is Blind

Look before You Leap

Ask the class the following questions:

Who or what are the two characters in the illustration? Can you describe their heads, bodies, and legs? How would you say that they are feeling toward each other? What makes you think so? Do you find the two characters attractive or unattractive? Can you say why? Do you think the two characters find each other attractive? Why? Do you believe that they would make good pets? Can you say why or why not?

Make Hay While the Sun Shines

Ask the class the following questions:

The two characters in the picture look like some kind of bugs. Can you name other common bugs? Most bugs are considered pests. Can you say why? What other pests can you name? In which ways are they troublesome? Do you think that your taste is shared by many other people? Why or why not? Have you ever found someone attractive that seemed rather ordinary to your friends? What was it in this person that you found attractive? Why do you think your friends did not agree with you? Do you believe that attraction for another person can be both physical and intellectual? Explain why or why not. Do you forgive people readily or do you hold grudges? Comment. When two people like one another, do you think that they can see each other's shortcomings? In your opinion do they tend to overlook them? Comment. Does a bad habit in another person annoy you? How do you react? Do you believe that with the passing of time, one's faults can become more evident and constitute a source of annoyance? Comment. Does it seem to you that it is possible for two people to "fall out of love" because of faults that they see in each other? Comment on why or why not.

A Friend Who Shares . . .

Present this situation to the students for discussion:

No one had ever been able to understand why such a pretty young girl like Yvette could have fallen in love with a man who was so much stouter and shorter than she was. He didn't even have a steady source of income! They eventually ended up getting married. How can you explain her attraction for him?

Nothing Ventured, Nothing Gained

Have the students compose (orally or in writing) a speech or monologue based on the following situation:

When Ludmilla first saw Andre at a school orientation meeting for new students, she was immediately attracted to him. During the course of the semester they got to know each other quite well. Ludmilla could not help noticing that Andre was very untidy and had some annoying personal habits. In spite of this, she felt herself drawn closer to him, and soon she had eyes for no one else.

Practice Makes Perfect

I. Select the proverb that best fits each situation.

1. When I lost my home in that fire, Maria invited me to stay with her. Her apartment is small, but she shared everything she had with me.
   a. Beauty is in the eye of the beholder.
   b. Imitation is the sincerest form of flattery.
   c. A friend who shares is a friend who cares.

2. Castille is my best friend, but when he accused my sister Sylvia of lying, I had to stand by Sylvia.
   a. Love is blind.
   b. Familiarity breeds contempt.
   c. Blood is thicker than water.

3. When Hui left on his business trip, I was looking forward to some time alone. But now I really miss him.
   a. Absence makes the heart grow fonder.
   b. A friend in need is a friend indeed.
   c. Blood is thicker than water.

4. Tai told me she wants to be a plumber when she grows up. When I asked her why, she said, "Because that's what you are, mommy."
   a. Imitation is the sincerest form of flattery.
   b. A friend who shares is a friend who cares.
   c. Familiarity breeds contempt.

5. When the basement flooded last month, my friend Irena came over and helped me clean everything up.
   a. A friend who shares is a friend who cares.
   b. A friend in need is a friend indeed.
   c. Beauty is in the eye of the beholder.

6. I can't understand why Paolo keeps that rusty old sculpture in front of his house.
   a. Blood is thicker than water.
   b. Beauty is in the eye of the beholder.
   c. Imitation is the sincerest form of flattery.

7. You try working with Tom for twenty years, and then you'll know why I don't like him.
   a. Familiarity breeds contempt.
   b. A friend who shares is a friend who cares.
   c. Love is blind.

8. Huimei doesn't seem to notice that her husband is loud and arrogant.
   a. Familiarity breeds contempt.
   b. Love is blind.
   c. Absence makes the heart grow fonder.

II. Complete the paragraphs with proverbs from the list below. Make changes in capitalization and punctuation as needed.

absence makes the heart grow fonder
beauty is in the eye of the beholder
blood is thicker than water
familiarity breeds contempt
a friend in need is a friend indeed
a friend who shares is a friend who cares
imitation is the sincerest form of flattery
love is blind

1. Did you see that awful painting in Floyd's living room? I guess _____ .

2. Thank you so much for giving me half your sandwich. I was really hungry.

   _____ .

3. Frank is hoping that Moira will get home from her business trip soon. They had an argument

   before she left. But you know, _____ .

4. Carlos and Ho Chu aren't speaking to each other these days. They've been neighbors for twenty-

   five years, and they think _____ .

5. Tanya came over the minute she heard about my accident. It's true that _____ .

6. Some people say that Marta is snobbish. Maybe _____ , but I think they are
   wrong.

7. I don't care how long we've been friends, I won't side with you against my brother.

   _____ .

8. It is said that _____ . If so, my friends must really like me. They are all getting
   their hair cut just like mine.

III. Complete the crossword puzzle using the clues below.

Across

1. _____ breeds contempt

4. blood is _____ than water

6. _____ is blind

7. a friend in need is _____

8. imitation is the _____ of flattery

Down

2. _____ is a friend who cares

3. beauty is _____ the beholder

5. _____ makes the heart grow fonder

Answer Key

I. 1. c.
    2. c.
    3. a.
    4. a.
    5. b.
    6. b.
    7. a.
    8. b.

II. 1. beauty is in the eye of the beholder
    2. A friend who shares is a friend who cares
    3. absence makes the heart grow fonder
    4. familiarity breeds contempt
    5. a friend in need is a friend indeed
    6. love is blind
    7. Blood is thicker than water
    8. imitation is the sincerest form of flattery

Crossword solution:

Across:
1. FAMILIARITY
4. THICKER
6. LOVE
(row) A FRIEND INDEED
8. SINCEREST FORM

Down:
2. AFRIENDWHOSHOSHA (A F R I E N D W H O S H A R E)
3. INTHEEYEOF
5. ABSENCE
7. RE

Grid letters:

1F 2A M 3I L I A R I T Y
    F   N
    R   4T H I C K E R
    I   H
    E   E
    N   E
    D   Y   5A
    W   E   B
    H   O   S
    O   F   6L O V E   E
    S   N
    H   C
    A F R I E N D I N D E E D
7R
    E
8S I N C E R E S T F O R M

Section Eight
Words to Live By

78.   Actions Speak Louder Than Words

Look before You Leap

Ask the class the following questions:

Can you describe the two men in the illustration? What does the younger man have in his hand? What is he doing with it? Why? How about the other guy? What do you suppose he was doing? Why? How are the two men different? What do you think they have in common? Who is the woman seated in the chair? Does it appear that she is equally attracted to both men? If not, for whom does she show a preference? Why? Which of the two men do you think will win her over? Why would you say so?

Make Hay While the Sun Shines

Ask the class the following questions:

A rose is a flower. Do you know the names of other flowers? On what occasions do people give flowers? Why do they give them? In your native country what flowers grow in abundance? Which ones are most popular? Why? How do flowers make you feel? Do you think that men and women feel the same way about receiving flowers? Explain. Have you ever tried to get somebody's attention? If so, how did you go about it? Do you think that a person is more impressed by words or by gifts? Comment. Can you describe how you feel when you receive a gift? Has anybody ever tried to talk you into doing something you didn't want to do? Were they successful? Describe the situation. How would you interpret the expression "All smoke and no fire"? Have you ever made a promise that you could not keep? If so, explain the circumstances and the reaction of the other person. Has anyone ever made a promise to you that he or she did not keep? How did you react? Would you ever believe that person again? Comment. Can you comment on what qualities in a person inspire trust?

A Friend Who Shares . . .

Present this situation to the students for discussion:

Although many of the members of the youth center would constantly complain about the refuse on the grounds surrounding the center, nobody had ever taken any action to get rid of it. One day the members of the swim club decided to take matters into their own hands and called for a clean-up party on a Saturday afternoon. Every member of the club showed up and the refuse was cleaned up in a matter of hours. What do you suppose the director of the center said to the other youth groups who complained and did nothing to improve the appearance of the grounds?

Nothing Ventured, Nothing Gained

Have the students compose (orally or in writing) a speech or monologue based on the following situation:

During a recent earthquake, many people were left destitute, and although there was a lot of talk about alleviating the situation no one seemed to be doing anything to help out. Finally, in desperation, the citizens of a hard-hit community formed a committee, elected a spokesperson, and went to the central authorities, demanding that something be done to help them out. Soon thereafter truckloads of food and medicine began arriving to the stricken area.

79. Better Late Than Never

Look before You Leap

Ask the class the following questions:

What kind of outfit does the man have on? How is it different from an ordinary suit? Why do you think he is wearing that type of suit? Where do you suppose he is? How do you think he got there? What is he doing? Would you say that he is enjoying himself? Do you believe that he would be able to do the same things on earth? Why or why not? Why do you suppose he is rushing? Does it appear that he will reach his destination on time? Explain.

Make Hay While the Sun Shines

Ask the class the following questions:

Do you know what an astronaut is? What do astronauts do? Why would they wear space suits? If you were on the moon, why would you need a space suit? Why can you jump higher on the moon than you can on earth? Do you consider yourself a punctual person? Have there ever been occasions when you were late in arriving for an appointment? If so, what happened? How about being late in completing an assignment? Comment. Can you describe your feelings when you do not do something on time? Do you ever tend to procrastinate? If so, explain on what occasions you might or might not procrastinate. In your opinion, does it make much difference if something is done late—as long as it gets done? Comment. Have you ever loaned anybody anything? Did you get back whatever you loaned within a specified period of time? Describe the occasion. If the person was late in returning what he or she had borrowed, how did you react? Would you ever trust that person again? Explain why you might or might not.

A Friend Who Shares . . .

Present this situation to the students for discussion:

Alberto felt terrible because he had forgotten his wife's birthday. He felt guilty and wanted to make amends. He went out and bought a big box of candy and a beautiful diamond necklace that his wife had once admired in the showcase window of a jewelry store. When he presented his wife with a belated birthday card and the presents, what do you think she said?

Nothing Ventured, Nothing Gained

Have the students compose (orally or in writing) a dialogue based on the following situation:

Ralph and Ned had had a dispute and because they were both so stubborn, neither one would admit he was wrong. The years went by and Ralph finally realized he was in error. He looked up his friend and apologized for being so hardheaded. Ned's feelings were assuaged and the two resumed their friendship.

80. Better Safe Than Sorry

Look before You Leap

Ask the class the following questions:

Where is the man going? Does he seem to be in a hurry? Explain. Can you describe the two roads depicted in the illustration? What do they have in common? In which ways are they different? Does it appear that one road is better than the other? Why do you suppose that the man chose one over the other? What are the advantages or disadvantages of the route that the man has chosen? Do you think that the man regrets his decision? Comment.

Make Hay While the Sun Shines

Ask the class the following questions:

What is a dangerous predicament? Have you ever been in one? Can you describe other dangerous situations? What makes them dangerous? Are you by nature a cautious person, or do you take risks? Describe under what circumstances you might exercise caution and under what circumstances you might want to take a risk. Can you name or describe different kinds of risks? Have you ever done something you ended up regretting? Can you describe the occasion? Did your course of action hurt you or another person? If so, how? Can you explain what is meant by the saying "Look before you leap"? Have you ever gone into a project without first investigating the pros and cons of the situation? If so, describe. Was the outcome favorable or unfavorable? Why? Do you believe that it is possible to be overcautious? In what type of situation might this be so? Comment. Do you think that people who are overcautious are apt to be indecisive? Explain why or why not. Within the realm of your experience would you say that a safe course of action will always ensure a favorable outcome?

A Friend Who Shares . . .

Present this situation to the students for discussion:

Conrad lived some distance from the playground and often took a shortcut to get there even though he had been warned that the shortcut ran through a rough, dangerous neighborhood. As his friend, you try to convince him to take an alternate, safer route even though it is longer. What might be one of the arguments you would use to convince him to take your advice?

Nothing Ventured, Nothing Gained

Have the students compose (orally or in writing) a speech or monologue based on the following situation:

Jobs had been hard to find, and after weeks of searching Lois finally obtained a position with one of the local business concerns. At first, she was excited about her new job. Unfortunately, it was not long before she became disenchanted with the working conditions and resolved to lodge some strong complaints with her immediate supervisor. However, when she thought about the scarcity of jobs she changed her mind. She came to the conclusion that she would be much better off not to say a word—at least, for now.

81.   A Bird in the Hand Is Worth Two in the Bush

Look before You Leap

Ask the class the following questions:

What does the man have in his arms? What kind does it look like? Does he appear satisfied with what he has? How is he holding it? Why? What is he looking for? Do the creatures in the bush seem to be afraid of the man? Can you explain why they would or would not have reason to fear him?

Make Hay While the Sun Shines

Ask the class the following questions:

In America what is the name of the bird traditionally served on Thanksgiving? In your native country is any type of bird served as the main course for a special occasion? If so, can you describe the occasion? Can you name other birds that are commonly used as food by humans? Are some birds more valuable than others? Can you say why? Where do birds live? How do they feed their young? Generally speaking, are you satisfied with your job? Can you say why or why not? Do you seek something better? If so, do you need any further training to obtain it? How about your status as a student? Can you describe what your plans are for the future? What do you need to accomplish to reach your goal? Have you ever tried to upgrade any of your possessions? If so, why? Were you successful? Explain the occasion. Do you think that the more one has, the more one wants? State your opinion and cite an occasion to illustrate. Are you willing to give up what you have in the hopes of getting something better? Explain why you feel as you do.

A Friend Who Shares... Present this situation to the students for discussion:

Aaron had been looking for a rare record by his favorite singer and happened to come across a copy in a record store. Although the copy was old and scratched, it was nevertheless quite expensive. Aaron wondered if he should put out the money for the record now, or if he should wait for a possible reissue in stereo, one with less surface noise. Knowing that the record might not ever be reissued, what would you suggest to Aaron?

Nothing Ventured, Nothing Gained Have the students compose (orally or in writing) a dialogue based on the following situation:

Mr. and Mrs. Lockwood were shopping for an antique dining-room set, and Mrs. Lockwood saw what she thought to be the perfect set in the first store they visited. She was on the point of buying it, when Mr. Lockwood intervened and said they should look around a little bit more. They visited a number of other stores, but found nothing that could compare with what they had first seen. When they went back to purchase it, the set was gone.

82. Charity Begins at Home

Look before You Leap Ask the class the following questions:

Who might the woman and the little girl be? What do they have in their hands? What are they asking for? Who is the man? Why do you think he is there? What is he doing? Do you think that he knows the lady and the little girl? Would you say that the man is concerned about their welfare? Does it appear that they are in need?

Make Hay While the Sun Shines Ask the class the following questions:

Can you make a distinction between generosity and charity? In what circumstances might a person need charity? Do you think that most people readily accept charity? Why or why not? In what different ways can a person show generosity? Is generosity shown only in a material way, or can it also be shown spiritually? Explain. Have you ever had to help out a close friend or acquaintance? In what way? Describe the other person's needs and how you came to be involved in the situation. Have you ever been in a position where you were in need? If so, describe the occasion. Did someone come to your aid? Was he or she able to help? What did this person do to make things easier for you? Can you describe ways in which a person can be charitable to people he or she does not know? Have you ever offered help in any way to someone less fortunate than you? If so, describe the occasion. What was the need? How were you able to help? What was the outcome? Do you believe that people should dedicate themselves exclusively to the needs of their immediate family and ignore the needs of others? Explain why you feel as you do.

A Friend Who Shares . . .

Present this situation to the students for discussion:

Lately, Mr. Hawkins had taken to going out with his friends for beers and relaxation after work. Mrs. Hawkins was stuck at home taking care of the house and the kids by herself. The burden had become excessive. One evening, when Mr. Hawkins arrived home after socializing with his friends, his wife reminded him of his obligations toward his own family. What do you think she said to him?

Nothing Ventured, Nothing Gained

Have the students compose (orally or in writing) a speech or monologue based on the following situation:

Pam was by nature a very giving, generous person. Although she was not wealthy, she did a lot of volunteer work for charitable organizations. One day while she was strolling through a shopping mall, a stylish, attractive suit caught her eye. As it turned out, the suit was rather expensive; nevertheless, she decided to pamper herself and bought the suit in spite of the high price. After all, since she unselfishly gave of her time to others, she figured it was her turn to be good to herself.

83.   Haste Makes Waste

Look before You Leap

Ask the class the following questions:

What do you think happened to the woman in the illustration? Does it seem to you that it was her fault? How might this have happened? Was she careless? What was she holding? What happened to them? Do you think that the whole incident could have been avoided if she had exercised more caution? Explain why or why not. Does it appear that she was in a hurry to get somewhere? Do you think that the woman could have done the same thing even under normal circumstances? Explain why or why not.

Make Hay While the Sun Shines

Ask the class the following questions:

Can you describe conditions that would cause someone to slip? When a person does slip and fall, what different things could happen to him or her? Have you ever had a fall? Under what conditions? Describe the incident. When one does a job in a hurry, do you think the quality of work will be the same as if that person had taken time to accomplish the task? Cite an incident where this may or may not be true. Can you recall an incident where you or someone you know has had to act in haste? Describe the incident. What was the outcome? Do you know what a deadline is? Have you ever had to meet one? Describe how you went about doing so. Was it orderly and systematic, or did you leave the bulk of the work for the last minute? Comment. Do you believe that if one does something in a slow deliberate manner he or she will accomplish the task without mishap? Cite an incident to illustrate your point of view. How about the opposite? Do you believe that when a person does something in a hurry, the outcome will always be an unfavorable one?

A Friend Who Shares . . .

Present this situation to the students for discussion:

Jack was down in the dumps about the final grade in one of his college courses. During the final exam, he was in such a hurry to finish that he did not pay close attention to the directions for completing a particular section. Because of his inattentiveness, he left out a lot of essential information in the essay. What did he realize too late?

Nothing Ventured, Nothing Gained

Have the students compose (orally or in writing) a dialogue based on the following situation:

Dora planned a dinner party for some of her women friends. Although she would be pressed for time, she felt that she could get everything ready when she came home from work. The main entree was to be fish, served with a special sauce. No sooner had she begun to prepare the sauce, when her guests started arriving. She welcomed her guests and returned momentarily to the kitchen to finish up the sauce. In her haste to get back to her guests she left out two essential ingredients that would have given the sauce its tangy, delicious flavor. Dora was made acutely aware of her omission when dinner was finally served. After having taken only one or two bites, most of her guests left the entire piece of fish on their plates!

84.   Love Makes the World Go Round

Look before You Leap

Ask the class the following questions:

What is in the center of the illustration? What is one bird doing to the other? Why? Where are they running? Does it appear that the bird being chased is afraid of the other bird? Explain. Do you think that the bird on the left wants to harm the other one? If not, what is the basis for your opinion? Why do you think that the two birds are running around the globe? Could their actions have a universal meaning? Give reasons for your opinion.

Make Hay While the Sun Shines

Ask the class the following questions:

The earth is one of the planets of our solar system. Can you name the others? Do you know what astrology is? Can you describe it? Do you think that many people believe in it? Do you believe that the position of the planets and stars can influence our lives? Comment. Based on your personal experiences, would you say that people born under a particular astrological sign all display personality characteristics that are attributed to that sign? Love is an emotion. Can you name ways in which one person can show love for another? Do you believe that love is fleeting or lasting? Is it a feeling that comes upon one suddenly, or must it be nurtured in order to grow? Comment on each of the above notions, and state reasons or give a specific incident to support your opinion. Do you believe that one gets what one gives? For example, if you are kind and considerate toward a human being or toward an animal, do you think that they will respond in kind? Comment by citing an occasion to illustrate your point of view.

A Friend Who Shares...

Present this situation to the students for discussion:

Mr. Carlson, who lived alone, had had a series of setbacks and was constantly down in the dumps. One day his next-door neighbor, a kind woman who had recently lost her husband, brought Mr. Carlson a cake to cheer him up. One thing led to another and pretty soon they were keeping steady company with each other. Life had now become bright and meaningful for both of them. What do you suppose their friends all said when they saw them both so happy and vibrant?

Nothing Ventured, Nothing Gained

Have the students compose (orally or in writing) a dialogue based on the following situation:

Mr. Foggerty enjoyed the reputation of being the town grump. One summer his niece, Larissa, came to visit him. She was by nature a kind, giving person who was always very loving and understanding with her uncle. She simply would not allow herself to be intimidated by his outbursts and short temper. To everyone's amazement, it was not long after Larissa's arrival that Mr. Foggerty began to say hello to people and even to smile at little children at play. It was just a matter of time before the people of the town reciprocated. They even invited him and his niece to the annual picnic and dance.

85. One Good Turn Deserves Another

Look before You Leap

Ask the class the following questions:

What is the man on the left doing? Describe the man in the middle. How is he dressed? What is he holding in his hand? Why? Does it appear that he is in need? Explain. Who is the man seated on the ground? What is he doing there? Describe him. How is he dressed? Would you say that he is in need? Explain. Do you think that he would be in any position to offer the type of help he is receiving? Why not?

Make Hay While the Sun Shines

Ask the class the following questions:

What is a favor? Can you name different kinds of favors? Can you explain the difference between a good deed and a favor? Do they have anything in common? Have you ever helped someone out? In which way? Did you do so voluntarily or were you asked to help? Did you expect something in return? Why or why not? In the course of everyday living, do you have occasion to ask people to do things for you? Comment. When someone grants you a small request, do you think that person expects repayment in kind? Explain. Can you describe an occasion where either you or someone you know needed help? Was the problem financial or mental? Who helped out? How? Did you or your friend feel obliged to repay the favor? Describe. Do you believe that a person is motivated to do someone a favor because he thinks that he will receive some sort of reward or a special favor in return? Can you cite situations where this might or might not occur?

A Friend Who Shares...

Present this situation to the students for discussion:

Fernando Suarez and Alicia Campos were students in a small university. They were both taking classes in math and English. Although Fernando was doing well in English, he was having trouble with math. Alicia, on the other hand, was brilliant in math but was having trouble with her English. While conversing casually, Fernando happened to mention his problem with math. Alicia immediately offered to tutor him. In exchange Fernando offered to help Alicia with her English assignments. Why would you say he did so?

Nothing Ventured, Nothing Gained

Have the students compose (orally or in writing) a speech or monologue based on the following situation:

Dwight had established a business that was quite successful. His friend, Sheldon, had been having some hard times and approached his friend for a loan to help him get back on his feet. Dwight had no hesitation in lending him the money he needed. Several years passed and they lost touch with each other. However, during this time Sheldon had managed to overcome his financial difficulties and had put away a significant amount of money in his savings account. Unfortunately, Dwight had a reversal of fortune and was now himself in need of financial aid. When he looked up his old friend and asked him if he was in a position to repay the loan, Sheldon not only repaid what he had borrowed, but included a hefty bonus in addition to the original amount.

86.   You Have to Take the Good with the Bad

Look before You Leap

Ask the class the following questions:

Can you identify the man on the left? How can you tell who he is? What about the three other tall men? What are they wearing? Who would you say they are? Can you describe the short man in the middle? What is he wearing? What does he have in his mouth? From all appearances, would you say that he belongs with the group? Explain why or why not. Why do you think that the man on the left is looking at him? How do you suppose he feels toward him? Why? Can you tell in which sport the men might be engaged? Does it appear that they would play well? Do you think that they would be happy playing with the shorter man? Why or why not? Explain.

Make Hay While the Sun Shines

Ask the class the following questions:

Do you know anything about football? Can you describe the sport? Is American football the same as European or South American football? Explain in which ways they are similar and in which ways they differ. Is football popular in your native country? Why do you think so many people are football enthusiasts? What do they find so appealing about the game? Can you comment on any negative elements of the game? Is it safe? Is it dangerous? What could happen? Have you ever counted on having something or doing something that did not work out for you? Describe the incident. How did you feel? Were you discouraged from trying again? Comment. Can you describe an incident that turned out well for you? Did everything go smoothly? Were there any disappointments along the way? Do you feel it difficult to adjust to a disappointment? How do you react when faced with a negative situation? Have you ever been faced with a problem that seemed difficult or impossible to solve? Did you give up trying to solve it? Why or why not? Have you ever lost a contest or competition? If so, can you describe the event? How did you react to defeat? Were you discouraged from renewing your efforts to do better next time? Comment.

A Friend Who Shares . . .

Present this situation to the students for discussion:

While shopping at the supermarket, Hugh saw a bag of apples that looked very enticing. It was selling for a good price, so he bought it. When he got home and opened the bag, he noticed that two or three of the apples were rotten. He apologized to his mom for spending the money, but she told him not to concern himself about it. What could she have said to him?

Nothing Ventured, Nothing Gained

Have the students compose (orally or in writing) a speech or monologue based on the following situation:

Leona couldn't make up her mind about her job. Should she stay, or should she leave? She liked her work, and the money was good. The only problem was her boss. He was rude and constantly reproached her for things that were not her fault. After much deliberation, she decided to stay and try to ignore her boss's comments. After all, jobs were hard to find and she needed a steady source of income.

87. You Reap What You Sow

Look before You Leap

Ask the class the following questions:

In what position is the man? What is he doing? Does it appear that he has been working hard? Where do you think he has been working? What is the name of the garden tool against the tree? What is it used for? Can you describe the man? Does he look energetic? Explain. From what you can see, would you say that the garden has been well taken care of? Why or why not? Does it appear that anything will grow in the garden? From all appearances, would you say that the man cares? Comment on why you think as you do.

Make Hay While the Sun Shines

Ask the class the following questions:

Do you know the names of any gardening tools? How are they used? Can you name any vegetables or flowers that grow in a garden? What do plants need to grow? Are you the type of person who is conscientious about what you do? If so, can you describe in what ways? For example, do you work hard at what you do? Do you complete assignments on time? Do you put things off? Do you believe that the harder one works, the better the results? Why or why not? Do certain things come easily to you? Explain. Can you attain good results with a minimum amount of effort? How about things that are harder to do? Do you think that good results can be attained with a lot of effort on your part? Explain why or why not. Can you describe an incident or occasion where you have derived some benefit as a result of something you did? Do you think that if one works hard he will necessarily be successful in the project he undertakes? Why or why not? Do you think that even if one works hard at something, it is possible that the benefits will not be as rewarding as one might expect? Comment on this question and cite examples or situations to illustrate, if possible.

A Friend Who Shares . . .

Present this situation to the students for discussion:

Isaac could speak very little English, but he knew that he had to have a good command of the language in order to succeed at a given profession in America. He studied hard and eventually became a famous surgeon. What might Isaac say to his son Sherman when Sherman tells him that he doesn't feel like doing his homework?

Nothing Ventured, Nothing Gained

Have the students compose (orally or in writing) a dialogue based on the following situation:

Jed was an ambitious, intelligent young man who did well in his studies. Unfortunately, he had a nasty habit of undercutting the accomplishments of his colleagues and of criticizing his professors. Upon graduation he applied for a position with a major business enterprise. In order to submit a complete application, he was required to furnish letters of recommendation attesting to his character and scholastic achievement. When Jed approached his former friends and teachers and asked them to help him out, they all declined, saying that they were too busy.

Practice Makes Perfect

I. Select the proverb that best fits each situation.

1. Our congressman often talks about how we must stop using automobiles as our primary method of transportation. But every day he drives his car the three blocks from his home to his office building.
    a. Actions speak louder than words.
    b. A bird in the hand is worth two in the bush.
    c. You reap what you sow.

2. Francoise works at the homeless shelter every night. She plays with the children and reads them stories. But she never seems to have time for her own children.
    a. One good turn deserves another.
    b. Charity begins at home.
    c. Haste makes waste.

3. Wing never took a vacation. He worked extra hours each week and saved all his money. Now Wing is taking a cruise around the world.
    a. Love makes the world go round.
    b. One good turn deserves another.
    c. You reap what you sow.

4. Zeno's dog barked all night long and kept Theresa awake. The next day Theresa visited Zeno and took him some cookies. During the visit she mentioned that Zeno's dog kept her awake all night. Zeno was so moved by Theresa's kindness and politeness that now he keeps his dog quiet every night.
    a. Better safe than sorry.
    b. Better late than never.
    c. Love makes the world go round.

5. Jeff was expecting his tax refund in April. It didn't come until August, but he was still very happy to get it.
    a. You reap what you sow.
    b. Better late than never.
    c. Actions speak louder than words.

6. Carla asked Judy to go to a play with her, but Judy didn't have enough money. Carla remembered that Judy bought her dinner one time last year, so Carla paid for Judy's theater ticket.
    a. One good turn deserves another.
    b. You have to take the good with the bad.
    c. Charity begins at home.

7. My cousin offered to give me his old computer. I might be able to get a newer one for free from Sandra's uncle. However, Sandra's uncle hasn't really offered it to me yet, so I will accept my cousin's offer.
    a. Haste makes waste.
    b. Better late than never.
    c. A bird in the hand is worth two in the bush.

8. My son's soccer team won three games in a row. Then yesterday they lost. I told him that he should accept losing just as he does winning.
   a. One good turn deserves another.
   b. You have to take the good with the bad.
   c. Better safe than sorry.

9. Reuben hurried to finish painting the bedroom so he could go fishing. But he splattered paint on the windows, and now he has to scrape them clean.
   a. Charity begins at home.
   b. Actions speak louder than words.
   c. Haste makes waste.

10. Eliza's car was making a strange sound, so she took it to a mechanic. She didn't know if there was really a problem, but she didn't want the car to break down while she was driving.
    a. Better safe than sorry.
    b. You have to take the good with the bad.
    c. Love makes the world go round.

II. Complete the dialogues with proverbs from the list below. Make changes in capitalization and punctuation as needed.

actions speak louder than words
better late than never
better safe than sorry
a bird in the hand is worth two in the bush
charity begins at home
haste makes waste
love makes the world go round
one good turn deserves another
you have to take the good with the bad
you reap what you sow

Dialogue 1

Hiroe: Are you going to the Environmental Group meeting tonight?

Grace: I don't know. I agree with all that ecology stuff, but do I have to go to the meetings?

Hiroe: Going to the meetings shows that you care. _____ .

Grace: I know that, but I need to spend more time with my husband. You know that

_____ .

Hiroe: True, but didn't the Environmental Group help solve that problem at your husband's factory? They helped you, so you should help them. _____ .

Grace: Well, maybe I'll bring my husband with me. He doesn't get off work until 6:30, so we'll be a little late.

Hiroe: That's okay. _____ .

Dialogue 2

    Alain: Did you see the latest memo from the boss?

    Jerald: Yes. She wants us to stick with the clients we know and not risk losing them for new clients, even if the new ones will bring us more money. She thinks that _____ .

    Alain: I think she's right. _____ .

    Jerald: I disagree. We need to consider new clients, or we'll be in trouble if we lose our old ones. If we ignore new clients now, they may ignore us later. _____ .

Dialogue 3

    George: Yesterday we sold all of our tomatoes, but today we can't seem to sell any.

    Mario: The vegetable business is like that. _____ .

    George: Aren't you upset that business is so bad today?

    Mario: No. No matter what kind of day I'm having, I try to greet my customers with a friendly smile. _____ .

    George: Come on, let's pack everything up and go home. I want to watch the game on TV.

    Mario: Be careful with those tomatoes! If you bruise them, no one will ever buy them. _____ .

III. Fill in the blanks below, then find and circle the missing words in the puzzle. Be sure to look horizontally, vertically, and diagonally.

1. _____ speak louder than words.

2. Better _____ than never.

3. Better safe than _____ .

4. A bird in the hand is worth _____ .

5. _____ begins at home.

6. Haste makes _____ .

7. Love makes _____ .

8. _____ deserves another.

9. You have to take _____ with the bad.

10. You reap _____ .

```
a  r  d  w  e  k  l  f  b  a  u  t  r  l  i
d  s  n  o  i  t  c  a  l  i  n  f  a  w  x
p  e  u  h  s  e  i  b  v  w  p  t  a  e  c
p  r  o  t  w  o  i  n  t  h  e  b  u  s  h
q  u  r  y  h  d  m  s  p  i  c  c  o  p  a
a  l  o  s  k  e  d  j  f  h  g  m  z  m  r
n  x  g  b  c  v  g  y  t  u  r  i  e  o  i
p  q  d  o  w  i  s  o  r  r  y  e  u  m  t
v  m  l  i  v  o  a  p  o  w  t  s  i  s  y
b  i  r  t  e  q  u  o  k  d  s  a  d  i  o
l  i  o  b  z  w  o  s  u  o  y  t  a  h  w
g  h  w  u  r  t  c  m  e  a  f  r  e  r  a
o  n  e  g  o  o  d  t  u  r  n  i  n  v  s
d  e  h  s  e  v  r  t  q  o  x  k  m  u  t
e  g  t  m  a  r  i  t  e  g  o  n  d  p  e
```

Answer Key

I.
1. a.
2. b.
3. c.
4. c.
5. b.
6. a.
7. c.
8. b.
9. c.
10. a.

II. **Dialogue 1**
Actions speak louder than words
charity begins at home
One good turn deserves another
Better late than never

Dialogue 2
a bird in the hand is worth two in the bush
Better safe than sorry
you reap what you sow

Dialogue 3
You have to take the good with the bad
Love makes the world go round
Haste makes waste

III.
1. Actions
2. late
3. sorry
4. two in the bush
5. Charity
6. waste
7. the world go round
8. One good turn
9. the good
10. what you sow

```
a  r  d  w  e  k  l  f  b  a  u  t  r  l  i
d  s  n  o  i  t  c  a  l  i  n  f  a  w  x
p  e  u  h  s  e  i  b  v  w  p  t  a  e  c
p  r  o  t  w  o  i  n  t  h  e  b  u  s  h
q  u  r  y  h  d  m  s  p  i  c  c  o  p  a
a  l  o  s  k  e  d  j  f  h  g  m  z  m  r
n  x  g  b  c  v  g  y  t  u  r  i  e  o  i
p  q  d  o  w  i  s  o  r  r  y  e  u  m  t
v  m  l  i  v  o  a  p  o  w  t  s  i  s  y
b  i  r  t  e  q  u  o  k  d  s  a  d  i  o
l  i  o  b  z  w  o  s  u  o  y  t  a  h  w
g  h  w  u  r  t  c  m  e  a  f  r  e  r  a
o  n  e  g  o  o  d  t  u  r  n  i  n  v  s
d  e  h  s  e  v  r  t  q  p  x  k  m  u  t
e  g  t  m  a  r  i  t  e  g  o  n  d  p  e
```

Section Nine

Some Things Never Change

88.   After the Feast Comes the Reckoning

Look before You Leap

Ask the class the following questions:

Who is the man seated at the table? Where is he? Can you describe him? What does he have around his neck? What was he doing? Would you say that he is satisfied? Explain. Does it appear that he is on a diet? Explain. What is beside the table? Who is the man standing beside him? What is he handing the man at the table? Do you think the man at the table is happy to get it? Why or why not? Do you think he will be surprised by what he sees?

Make Hay While the Sun Shines

Ask the class the following questions:

Do you know what a maitre d' is? Can you name some of his or her duties? Do you ever have occasion to eat out? If so, what type of restaurant do you prefer? Can you say why? Do you consider yourself a big eater? If so, do you put on a lot of weight? Have you ever been on a diet? Do you have trouble staying on it? Have you been successful in losing weight? If so, have you been able to keep it off? Do you know people who can eat what they want and still keep off the weight? Do you have any idea what factors might account for this? Can you name different types of excesses? Have you ever indulged in any excesses? If so, describe them. Can you say what usually happens to a person when he or she overeats or overworks? How about the use of credit? Do you have any credit cards? Do you use them wisely? Explain. Have you ever made a purchase that put a strain on your budget? If so, what was it? Did you have difficulty in paying it off? Describe the situation and the final outcome.

A Friend Who Shares . . .

Present this situation to the students for discussion:

Your friend Ian was invited to a banquet. After the banquet he comes to you and tells you that he has a stomachache because he overate. Of course you feel sorry for him, but at the same time what do you tell him to keep in mind?

Nothing Ventured, Nothing Gained

Have the students compose (orally or in writing) a speech or monologue based on the following situation:

Gunther had just been accepted into a fraternity. While attending a frat party, he had a bit too much to drink. Needless to say, the next morning he woke up with a gigantic hangover!

89.   Bad News Travels Fast

Look before You Leap

Ask the class the following questions:

Can you describe the man in the illustration? How is he dressed? Who is he? Why might he be dressed the way he is? What happened to him? How would you say he is feeling? Is he the only one who knows about his mishap? Explain. Do you think he will get into any trouble as a result of what happened? Why or why not?

Make Hay While the Sun Shines

Ask the class the following questions:

Can you name different ways that news or information is made available to the public? In your opinion, is it always accurate? Comment on your feelings. Do you believe everything you hear, see, or read in the media? Explain why or why not. Do you think that newscasters and journalists tend to exaggerate or "slant" the news? Can you support your opinion with reference to any concrete incident? What type of news do you suppose interests people the most?

Explain and give reasons for your opinion. Generally speaking, when you read the newspapers, what type of news would you say predominates? Why might this be so? What interests you the most—someone's good fortune or someone's misfortune? Explain why. In your opinion, would you say that news is as entertaining as it is informative? Do you think it is both? Explain, citing a situation or incident to support your opinion. Which do you believe travels faster—good news or bad news? Why?

A Friend Who Shares...   Present this situation to the students for discussion:

It was only a short time before the entire world knew about the death of a renowned humanitarian. Can you explain how everybody found out so quickly about the death?

Nothing Ventured, Nothing Gained   Have the students compose (orally or in writing) a speech or monologue based on the following situation:

The board of directors of a major corporation had made a decision to close down one of its local plants and to move its operations to another location. Many people would lose their jobs. Within minutes of the decision, the news spread like wildfire throughout the entire compound.

90. The Best Things in Life Are Free

Look before You Leap   Ask the class the following questions:

Where is the woman standing? What is she doing? What does she see? Describe her view. How would you describe her emotional state? How can you tell? Do you think that other people might enjoy doing the same thing? Explain why or why not. Is this an experience that she would want to share with others? Why or why not?

Make Hay While the Sun Shines   Ask the class the following questions:

Scenes of nature can be a source of great beauty. Can you describe some such scenes? Do you think that what is a source of joy to one person is necessarily a source of joy to another? Comment on your feelings. What things do you enjoy doing? Can you explain why? Can you describe some forms of entertainment? Does it cost money to enjoy them? Can you think of things that one might enjoy doing without cost? If you were asked to state your priorities, what would you consider the best things in life? Would they be expensive? Explain. Do you think that material goods give a person the most happiness? Explain why or why not. Arrange the foolowing order of importance: a) a happy marriage; b) financial independence; c) a beautiful sunset; d) love and respect of one's family and friends; e) a big house with a swimming pool; and f) good health. Give reasons for your choice.

A Friend Who Shares...   Present this situation to the students for discussion:

If you enjoyed good health and the love of your family and friends but had very little money, what could you say about your position in life?

**Nothing
Ventured,
Nothing Gained**

Have the students compose (orally or in writing) a dialogue based on the following situation:

Rather than spend their hard-earned money on a vacation at a fancy resort, Mr. and Mrs. Jacobs decided to stay at home and do things that they had never had the time to do before. They were truly excited about being tourists in their own town and not having to pay any expensive hotel bills.

91.   The Bigger They Are, the Harder They Fall

**Look before You
Leap**

Ask the class the following questions:

Can you identify the young boy? How is he dressed? What does he have in his hand? What do you suppose he did with it? What makes you think so? Who is lying on the ground? How would you describe him? Does he appear to be vanquished? How can you explain the fact that a smaller, weaker person could prevail over someone bigger and stronger?

**Make Hay While
the Sun Shines**

Ask the class the following questions:

Have you ever been in a competition where strength was a factor? Were you evenly matched with your opponent? What was the outcome? Who won—the stronger of the two or the most astute of the two? Describe the situation. Do you think that the bigger a person is, the stronger he or she is? Explain why or why not. Do you think that strength is strictly a physical attribute? If not, in what other ways can strength be shown? Can you name some ways in which a person can acquire power? Do you believe that powerful people are not vulnerable to failure or hurt? Explain your point of view. Have you ever failed in an endeavor? Describe the situation. What was the project? Did you experience successes along the way? What was the eventual outcome? Was it successful, or did it turn out badly? How did you feel? Discuss your experience. Do you believe that the reaction to failure of an important person is more acute than that of a person in a lesser position? Explain the reasons for your opinion.

**A Friend Who
Shares . . .**

Present this situation to the students for discussion:

When a big Hollywood star ended up on the streets because of a drinking problem, what do you suppose people were saying about him?

**Nothing
Ventured,
Nothing Gained**

Have the students compose (orally or in writing) a speech or monologue based on the following situation:

Because of his height and athletic build, Ken had no problem in making the gymnastic team. At the beginning of the season he showed great promise; however, he kept missing practice sessions. When it came time to compete for the regional gymnastic championship, Ken received the lowest score of any of the participants.

92.   Good Things Come in Small Packages

**Look before You
Leap**

Ask the class the following questions:

What is in the box on the floor? What is coming out of the box? Can you describe it? What would you say is so special about it? Could it have any supernatural powers? What might they be? How would you say the woman is feeling? Why? Do you think she would have been happier with a larger, more expensive package? Explain why or why not. Do you think that the person who presented the gift to the woman was aware of its value? Comment.

Make Hay While the Sun Shines

Ask the class the following questions:

Do you know what a genie is? Can you name things a genie is capable of doing? Where do genies usually live? Have you ever wished for something special? What was it? Did you get your wish? Describe the occasion. What are some of the things people wish for? Do you think that most people wish for material goods? What else might someone wish for? Do you believe that the bigger something is, the more valuable it is? Comment on why or why not. How about things that are small? Can they be of great value? If so, can you name some things that are? Do you know on what occasions people usually receive gifts? Do you think that the more expensive a gift is, the more it is appreciated? Comment. Can you describe a special gift that you received? Was it big or small? What was the occasion? When you saw the package what did you think? After you opened the package, did you like its contents? Comment. Have you ever received a gift with which you were disappointed? If so, what was the occasion? Can you say why you were disappointed? Describe the incident.

A Friend Who Shares...

Present this situation to the students for discussion:

The mail carrier has just delivered the mail. When you go to pick it up, you see an official-looking envelope. Upon opening it you are elated to see that it contains a check for a sizable tax refund. What would you say?

Nothing Ventured, Nothing Gained

Have the students compose (orally or in writing) a dialogue based on the following situation:

Although Carlos showered his wife with expensive material gifts, he was hardly ever affectionate and seldom responded to her emotional needs. A simple hug or gesture of affection from her husband would have meant much more to her than any present he could have given her.

93. The Grass Is Always Greener on the Other Side of the Fence

Look before You Leap

Ask the class the following questions:

Where is the horse? What is it doing? Why do you suppose it is sticking its head through the fence? Does it appear that the only nourishment available to the horse is where it is now feeding? Can you think of any reasons why it would not want to feed in its own field? Why would it seek food elsewhere? Discuss your point of view.

Make Hay While the Sun Shines

Ask the class the following questions:

Can you name some animals that graze in a pasture? What nourishment do these animals provide for man? Have you ever had occasion to be dissatisfied with something? If so, what was it? A job? A possession? State the reasons for your dissatisfaction. Do you think that people tend to want what they cannot have? Comment on why or why not, citing examples drawn from your personal observations. Have you ever been impressed by another person's accomplishments? If so, explain the situation. Can you explain your feelings when you see someone who, from all appearances, is better off than you? Would you want what he or she has? Why or why not? Do you think you might have some things other people might want? Think about your home, family, job, friends, material possessions, etc., and comment accordingly. Are you dissatisfied with your present position in life? Explain why or why not. Would you want to change anything? Do you think that something that looks good is necessarily as good as it appears? Comment.

A Friend Who Shares . . .

Present this situation to the students for discussion:

Jodi and Maurice had been inseparable for some time, and Jodi had no reason to think that Maurice would run off with someone else. But one day Maurice left Jodi and began seeing a woman from his health club. Why do you think he did so?

Nothing Ventured, Nothing Gained

Have the students compose (orally or in writing) a speech or monologue based on the following situation:

Marsha and Troy had been living in a big, old Victorian house for a number of years. One day, when they went to visit friends who had a new, modern home in the suburbs, both Marsha and Troy wanted one like it. They sold their house, bought a new one in the suburbs, and moved away from their old neighborhood and friends. As it turned out, the newer home lacked the character and appeal of the one they sold, and their new neighbors were distant and unfriendly. It was not long before Troy and Marsha regretted their move.

94.   Hindsight Is Better Than Foresight

Look before You Leap

Ask the class the following questions:

Can you describe the people in the illustration? How is the woman dressed? What is she carrying in her left arm? Why? What's the weather like? How about the men? How are they dressed? What does one of them have over his head? Why? Do you think that it will provide him adequate protection against the elements? Why do you suppose the men are clutching their coats? Judging from the looks on their faces, can you describe how they must be feeling? How about the woman? From all appearances, would you say that any of the three knew ahead of time what the weather was going to be like? Explain. What do you suppose they would have done had they known?

Make Hay While the Sun Shines

Ask the class the following questions:

Can you describe different types of inclement weather? What other expressions of weather do you know? What is the weather like in your native country? Can you name the four seasons? In the United States, what is the weather like during each of the four seasons? How about in your native country? Do you think that people stay indoors when it is very hot or very cold? If not, in what activities to do they engage? Before undertaking a project, do you examine all its aspects? Can you name a project that you have undertaken, and what preparations you made for it? How did it turn out? Do you think that careful planning always pays off? Why or why not? Have you ever done something that did not turn out well for you? Can you say why? Was it because of something you did, or was it because something happened that you could not foresee? Do you think it is possible to determine with certainty the outcome of a project? Why or why not? Have you ever walked into a troublesome situation with your eyes wide open? If so, describe the occasion. Did you learn what precautions to take so that the same thing would not happen to you in the future? Discuss the outcome of the incident.

A Friend Who Shares... Present this situation to the students for discussion:

When Emery received a low grade on his physics exam, he regretted the fact that he had not studied harder before he took it. He knew that he could have scored much higher if only he had taken the time to go over the material thoroughly and conscientiously.

Nothing Ventured, Nothing Gained Have the students compose (orally or in writing) a dialogue based on the following situation:

When Mr. and Mrs. Rosemond went out for the evening, they failed to lock the back door of their house. When they got back they were horrified to discover that during their absence a burglar had carried away many of their valuables. If only they had remembered to bolt the door before leaving, the whole thing could have been avoided.

95. It Never Rains but It Pours

Look before You Leap Ask the class the following questions:

Why do you think that the man and the woman are holding on to each other? What happened to the roof of their house? Who is running out of the house? What does he have over his shoulder? What do you suppose is in the bag? Do you know what the word *quarantined* means? Why is there a sign on the couple's door? What must have happened? Can you describe the windows above the doorway? Would you say that the mishaps depicted in the illustration happened over an extended period of time? Explain. Can you think of any other mishaps that could possibly occur?

Make Hay While the Sun Shines Ask the class the following questions:

Under what conditions might a quarantine be imposed? Can you name any illnesses that would require the patient to be placed in isolation? Why would isolation be necessary? Have you ever had a streak of bad luck? Can you can describe the series of events that took place? How did you handle the situation? Did things eventually turn around for you? Explain. Have you ever had a streak of good luck? Can you describe what happened? How long did your luck hold out? Comment. Do you believe that things occur in cycles? Comment on this notion, citing either a personal experience or the experience of someone you know. Once a series of mishaps begins to take place, do you think that anything can be done to break the chain? Do you believe that a person has control over his or her destiny? If so, to what extent? If not, why not? Comment on your point of view.

A Friend Who Shares... Present this situation to the students for discussion:

What comment could you make to a friend who informed you that in addition to winning a new car in a drawing, he was about to receive a substantial inheritance check from the estate of a relative who recently passed away?

Nothing Ventured, Nothing Gained Have the students compose (orally or in writing) a speech or monologue based on the following situation:

While Marisa and Dino were driving back home after a dinner party, they suddenly heard a loud bang, and their car began to swerve on the road. It was a flat tire! Dino managed to pull over to the side of the road and replaced the flat with the spare. No sooner had they set off on their way then they had to stop again because the engine started to overheat! They wondered what else could happen, and if they'd ever make it home.

96. Lightning Never Strikes Twice in the Same Place

Look before You Leap

Ask the class the following questions:

Can you describe the man on the left? What do you suppose happened to him? How about the guy on the right? What is happening to him? Do you think that he knew that he was placing himself in a dangerous position by standing on the mound? Explain. Do you think that what happened to the two men is a common occurrence? If not, why not? Does it appear that the man on the left is any the worse for his experience? If not, why not? If so, in which way? How about the man on the mound? Do you think he will survive the force of the impact? Comment. Do you think that either of the two men are likely to experience the same mishap at some future date? Explain why or why not.

Make Hay While the Sun Shines

Ask the class the following questions:

Besides lightning, what other natural occurrences can cause damage or pose great danger to humans and animals? Are thunderstorms common in your native country? If so, do they usually cause a great deal of damage? What manifestations of nature can have an adverse effect on the well-being of the population of a particular geographical location? Consider drought, flooding, snowstorms, tornadoes, etc., and comment on the effects of each. Are the effects catastrophic? Are you, or anyone you know, accident-prone? If so, can you describe the types of accident and how they came about? A number of professions are extremely dangerous. Can you name some of them and describe what might happen to people enegaged in these professions? Can you define the word *chance?* Do you think that some types of accidents are apt to occur with more frequency than others? Comment. Do you know what a freak accident is? Have you ever been in or witnessed a freak accident? If so, describe the circumstances. Describe the chances of such a thing happening to the same person a second time.

A Friend Who Shares...

Present this situation to the students for discussion:

Imagine that a friend of yours informed you that she won a big prize in a lottery. Because she won once, she feels certain that she can win again. So she goes out and buys more tickets. What would you remind her of?

Nothing Ventured, Nothing Gained

Have the students compose (orally or in writing) a dialogue based on the following situation:

One sunny afternoon, Teresa and her friend Laura decided to go shopping downtown. While the girls were walking along the sidewalk Teresa suddenly let out a yell. Without warning she had been hit on the head by a small piece of glass that evidently fell from one of the buildings. Although shaken, she was fortunately not hurt. Naturally, Teresa wanted to get out of the area as fast as possible. Her friend was able to calm her down by pointing out that it was a freak accident and that such a thing would probably never happen to her again.

97. Might Makes Right

Look before You Leap

Ask the class the following questions:

What is the man holding? Although not all of him can be seen, what do you imagine the man must be like? Can you give a fairly detailed description? Upon what do you base your description? Can you describe the instrument he is holding? What is attached on each side of the fulcrum? What are they used for? What would the arrow in the middle of the fulcrum indicate? Does one side appear to be heavier than the other? If not, what might the role of the man be? Is he in any way controlling the situation? Explain.

Make Hay While the Sun Shines

Ask the class the following questions:

Can you discuss for what purpose a scale such as that depicted in the illustration is used? Do you think such scales are currently in use? If so, where? If not, why not? Has something else replaced them? Do you know what a bully is? Have you or one of your friends ever been intimidated by one? Can you describe the occasion? Can you think of instances where someone has imposed his or her will on others because of superior strength or military might? Describe the situation and the reaction of the conquered party or parties. In your opinion, are there other ways—besides physical force—that a person can display his or her strength? Can you comment on situations where this is so? (Consider moral support and strength in the face of adversity.) Do you believe that a person of small stature can have great physical strength? Explain how this might or might not be so. Do you think that women can be as strong as men? If so, in what ways? Can you think of ways that one may gain the upper hand when one is faced with a show of force or brute strength?

A Friend Who Shares...

Present this situation to the students for discussion:

Jack, a strapping young man of 6'4", was getting into his car in a deserted parking lot when he was accosted by a scrawny robber who, holding a gun to Jack's head, demanded all of his money. Of course, Jack did not hesitate to comply with his assailant's demand. How do you explain the fact that Jack gave in so readily?

Nothing Ventured, Nothing Gained

Have the students compose (orally or in writing) a speech or monologue based on the following situation:

Alexy and Vera were opponents in the race for president of the student body of their school. Although Alexy had managed to amass a substantial number of supporters for advocating a broader sports program, it was Vera, with her platform of expanding the counseling services and the academic program of the school, that drew the biggest group of supporters. She won the presidency in a landslide!

98. No News Is Good News

Look before You Leap

Ask the class the following questions:

What is the woman watching? Why? Would you say that she is more interested in watching her favorite soap opera or the daily news? Why do you think she is standing rather than sitting? Does it appear that she is aware of what is happening around her? What would she have to do to find out? Can you describe the scene outside the window? Does the woman appear in any imminent danger? Why? Does she seem to be aware of her situation? What do you think she would do if she looked out the window?

Make Hay While the Sun Shines

Ask the class the following questions:

Can you name some of the sources that keep the public informed of what is happening locally and around the world? Do you think that the reporting is objective and accurate? Explain. From where do you get your information if you want to find out what is going on with family, relatives, or friends? Can you explain the saying "Ignorance is bliss"? Can you comment on how a person might react to good news? How about his or her reaction to bad news? If something bad is happening to a family member or friend, would you want to know about it right away, or would you rather not know anything until after it has occurred? Explain your reasoning. Some news is considered good, whereas some is considered bad. Can you list situations that would be considered good news and others that would be considered bad news? If you happen to be living far from a family member or friend, do you ever become concerned about his or her welfare if the two of you have not communicated in a long time? Explain why or why not.

A Friend Who Shares...

Present this situation to the students for discussion:

A good friend of yours applied for a position with an architectural firm. She's been on pins and needles waiting to hear if she is even being considered for the position. After recommending that she be patient, what would you remind her of?

Nothing Ventured, Nothing Gained

Have the students compose (orally or in writing) a speech or monologue based on the following situation:

Because of political and economic turmoil in her own country, Ala and her children had immigrated to another country. Unfortunately, Ala's husband had to stay behind to take care of some business matters and to dispose of the family's personal property. Although Ala knew that the postal service of her country was bad, she became quite worried when two months passed without a word from her husband. Her friends lent moral and financial support and reminded her that the absence of mail did not necessarily indicate a problem back home.

99.   Nothing Hurts like the Truth

Look before You Leap

Ask the class the following questions:

Where is this scene taking place? Can you describe the participants? For example, who is the man on the left? What is his role? Who are the three women seated next to him? What are they doing? Would you say that they are feeling friendly toward the man at the table? Explain. How about the man who is standing on the right? Who might he be? Can you describe him? How would you say he is feeling? Why? Can you describe the man seated at the table? Does he seem to be comfortable? What reason would he have for feeling the way he does?

Make Hay While the Sun Shines

Ask the class the following questions:

Can you say why a person might need a lawyer? What do you know about the judicial system of the United States? How does it compare with the judicial system of your native country? Have you ever heard of the expression "Justice is blind"? Can you explain what it means? Have you or someone you know ever been accused of wrongdoing? If so, comment on the occasion. Were you falsely accused? What were the grounds for the accusation? What was the outcome? In your opinion, was the cause of justice served? In the United States people believe that a person is innocent until proven guilty. From what you have seen or experienced, do you believe this to be true? Comment. Do you think that punishing a person for a crime will deter others from committing similar crimes? Explain why or why not, citing examples to support your position. Have you ever given any thought to the positive or negative side of your personality or character? What do you think are some of your positive traits? Can you see any negative traits within yourself? Comment. Can you describe what your reaction would be if someone brought to your attention an unpleasant truth about your behavior or appearance? Would you deny or admit it? Would you make any effort to overcome the problem? Comment. Have you ever had occasion to reproach anyone for doing something that annoyed you? Describe the occasion and the other person's reaction to your comment. The expression "If the shoe fits, wear it" is quite commonly heard. Can you say under what circumstances one might have the occasion to say it?

A Friend Who Shares . . .   Present this situation to the students for discussion:

Lately, Marcus had been lax in fulfilling his obligations at work. He received a negative evaluation. When he read it and was faced with the truth about his substandard performance on the job, he became terribly upset. Can you say why?

Nothing Ventured, Nothing Gained   Have the students compose (orally or in writing) a speech or monologue based on the following situation:

Wilma was a beautiful, friendly person until she went on a diet. She overdid it, and as a result she became too thin and her looks faded. Wilma's friends pointed out these changes to her. At first she resented their comments but after thinking about it, she realized that what they were saying about her was true. She thereupon decided to go off her diet and to keep her weight in check through exercise and sensible eating habits.

100.   Possession Is Nine-Tenths of the Law

Look before You Leap   Ask the class the following questions:

What two animals are depicted in the illustration? Where is one of the animals concealed? Do you think it belongs to the animal whose head is poking out? What do you suppose it might be doing there? Would you say that this is its natural habitat? If not, where might it feel more at home? How about the animal on the right? Can you describe it? What does its facial expression tell you about how it is feeling? Does it seem happy? Explain. What do you think it wants? Does it appear that it will get this? Comment on why or why not.

Make Hay While the Sun Shines   Ask the class the following questions:

Turtles carry their home on their backs. Can you name other animals or types of fish that live in a shell? Are any of them used as food for man? Do you know how turtles get around? Explain. How about foxes? Do they move quickly or slowly? Do you think that a fox would want to possess anything that a turtle has? Do you have any prized possessions? Can you name some of them and say why they are special? When you were younger, did you ever have to share any of your toys with a brother or sister? Did you do so willingly? Explain. Have you ever lost or misplaced anything of value? What was it? Did it have special meaning for you? How did you feel about the loss? Did you get it back? If so, comment on the circumstances of your loss and the eventual re-covery of your possession. Have you or someone you know ever found any-thing of value? If so, describe the occasion. State what you found and when and where you found it. Did you keep what you found or did you make some effort to get it back to its owner? Was it finally reclaimed? If so, how did you feel about giving it up? What was the reaction of the owner? Can you describe some things that one can do to find the owner of lost property? Besides things such as jewelry or other tangible objects, what other possessions of value to the owner could be lost? How would you feel about keeping something that you found if no one appeared to reclaim it? What would you do if the owner appeared to reclaim it at a later date? Can you comment on the meaning of the expression "Finders keepers, losers weepers"?

A Friend Who Shares...

Present this situation to the students for discussion:

Some kids were playing softball when one of them hit the ball over a fence, into a neighbor's yard. When he went over to reclaim the ball, the neighbor refused to hand it over, saying that it now belonged to her. How could the neighbor justify the fact that she kept the ball?

Nothing Ventured, Nothing Gained

Have the students compose (orally or in writing) a speech or monologue based on the following situation:

The authorities had a hard time trying to evict a group of homeless people who had occupied and laid claim to an old, abandoned building. The occupants claimed that because the building had been empty and they were the first to oc-cupy it, they had every right to continue living there.

101.   The Proof of the Pudding Is in the Eating

Look before You Leap

Ask the class the following questions:

What is on the table? Can you describe the man behind the table? What is he doing? Why? Who might he be? How can you tell? Does he seem to be enjoy-ing his task? What makes you think so? Why do you suppose he is there? What's the occasion? What factors do you think he will consider before ren-dering a decision?

Make Hay While the Sun Shines

Ask the class the following questions:

Contests are very popular in the United States. Can you name different types of contests? Are contests a part of the culture of your country? If so, describe some of these contests. Do you think there is any difference between a contest and a competition? Comment. If you were judging a beauty contest, upon which factors would you base your judgment? How about a contest for the most outstanding pie or cake? Are there some foods that you do not like? If so, what are they? Why don't you like them? Do you believe that one can develop a taste for certain foods or beverages? Have you ever done so? Comment. Do you think that there are certain foods that most people find tasty? If so, name some of them. How about foods that have little taste appeal? What might some of these be? Can you comment on the role that geography and climate have on cuisine? Did you have any difficulty in adjusting to American cuisine? Comment. Can you point out some of the differences between the cuisine of your native country and the cuisine of America? Do you think that the culture of a country plays a role in determining the diet of its people? Do you believe that the taste of certain dishes may be enhanced if they are artfully prepared and pleasant to behold? Comment on your opinion.

A Friend Who Shares . . .

Present this situation to the students for discussion:

Imagine that you know a person who has a reputation for not keeping his word. If this person wanted you to believe that he would fulfill a certain promise or obligation to you within a specified period of time, what could you say to him to show him that you would believe him only when he actually followed through?

Nothing Ventured, Nothing Gained

Have the students compose (orally or in writing) a speech or monologue based on the following situation:

It was a well-known fact that Mariana possessed a true gift for baking. Her specialty was cheesecake. One afternoon she invited some friends over for an informal gathering and served an artfully decorated cheesecake with coffee. Although she was in a hurry to prepare it since she had been running errands all morning long, she nevertheless managed to get it ready by the time her guests had arrived. It looked absolutely delicious, but hardly a person touched it after the first bite. Mariana was devastated. After her guests left, she tasted the cheesecake herself, and to her dismay she discovered that she had left out the sugar and sour cream! She thereupon took a vow never again to be in a hurry when preparing a baked delicacy.

Practice Makes Perfect

I. Select the proverb that best fits each situation.

1. Nathan's proposal is better than Elmer's, but Elmer has powerful friends on the administrative board. Elmer's proposal was adopted.
   a. Might makes right.
   b. After the feast comes the reckoning.
   c. The proof of the pudding is in the eating.

2. If I had known that I would need math skills in this business, I would have taken more math courses in college.
   a. Hindsight is better than foresight.
   b. It never rains but it pours.
   c. Good things come in small packages.

3. Go ahead and sign up for it! You'll never know if you like welding unless you try it.
   a. No news is good news.
   b. The proof of the pudding is in the eating.
   c. Nothing hurts like the truth.

4. My mother just called me from Greece. She had heard that my company went bankrupt. How did she find out? It only happened yesterday!
   a. The best things in life are free.
   b. Bad news travels fast.
   c. The bigger they are, the harder they fall.

5. Murray gave me a tiny little box for my birthday. Inside it was a diamond ring!
   a. The grass is always greener on the other side of the fence.
   b. Good things come in small packages.
   c. Lightning never strikes twice in the same place.

6. Melvin never does any work around here. He is always reading magazines or walking around. He is having a good time now, but someday Ms. Leach will find out what's going on. Then Melvin will be in big trouble.
   a. After the feast comes the reckoning.
   b. Nothing hurts like the truth.
   c. Possession is nine-tenths of the law.

7. I was caught speeding on this road yesterday, but the police won't be looking for speeders in the same place again today.
   a. The proof of the pudding is in the eating.
   b. Bad news travels fast.
   c. Lightning never strikes twice in the same place.

8. Marcia told me I was selfish. That made me very angry, but I guess she was right.
   a. No news is good news.
   b. Hindsight is better than foresight.
   c. Nothing hurts like the truth.

9. Phil was our congressman for fourteen years. He was a very important man in Washington. But after that tax scandal, Phil was thrown out of office in disgrace.
   a. The bigger they are, the harder they fall.
   b. It never rains but it pours.
   c. The best things in life are free.

10. I found that sack of money in my yard, and nobody is going to make me give it back to the bank.
    a. Possession is nine-tenths of the law.
    b. Nothing hurts like the truth.
    c. Might makes right.

11. Things would be a lot better for us if we moved to Tahiti.
    a. After the feast comes the reckoning.
    b. Bad news travels fast.
    c. The grass is always greener on the other side of the fence.

12. We had a wonderful time with the children on Saturday and we didn't spend any money! We just played in the park and talked about everything.
    a. The bigger they are, the harder they fall.
    b. Hindsight is better than foresight.
    c. The best things in life are free.

13. For months I couldn't get any work as a carpenter. Now, in the last few days, seven people have hired me to do remodeling work for them.
    a. Lightning never strikes twice in the same place.
    b. It never rains but it pours.
    c. Might makes right.

14. People are saying that the factory is going to lay off some workers soon. I haven't gotten any notices from the company, so I'm going to ignore the rumors.
    a. Good things come in small packages.
    b. No news is good news.
    c. The grass is always greener on the other side of the fence.

II. Match the situations in Column A with the proverbs in Column B.

	A	**B**
1.	I suppose we'll have to do it Brian's way. He has too much power for us to oppose him.	a. It never rains but it pours.
2.	If I had known that this house was built over an old coal mine, I never would have bought it.	b. Lightning never strikes twice in the same place.

3. Great vacations don't have to be expensive. Last summer I just stayed at home and played with my kids. It was one of my best vacations.

c. The bigger they are, the harder they fall.

4. Jake worked hard to get to the top of his field. His research made him famous. But now, reports of his improper research methods have ruined his reputation.

d. After the feast comes the reckoning.

5. Ed wouldn't move over so we could see the stage better. He said he got there first and it was his spot.

e. Bad news travels fast.

6. The literary critic said that Thelma's poetry was "shallow." Thelma is very upset because she knows that the critic is right.

f. Might makes right.

7. First my water heater leaks; then some shingles on my roof blow off; and now my oven doesn't work.

g. No news is good news.

8. The accountant said she would call me if there was a problem with my taxes. She hasn't called.

h. The proof of the pudding is in the eating.

9. Mario doesn't want to direct that new community program, but I told him he'll never know if he can direct a program unless he tries.

i. Possession is nine-tenths of the law.

10. Lalene and Bill rebuilt their house after a tornado hit it last summer. They say that they should be safe from tornadoes now.

j. Nothing hurts like the truth.

11. It was a small, ordinary envelope, but inside was a check for $10,000.

k. Hindsight is better than foresight.

12. I love staying up late to watch old movies on TV, but the next morning I always feel tired and irritable.

l. Good things come in small packages.

13. The Obikanes are moving again. Frank keeps changing jobs because new jobs always look better to him than his current job.

m. The best things in life are free.

14. —Did you hear that Sarah failed her algebra class?
    —Oh, sure. Everyone knows about it already.

n. The grass is always greener on the other side of the fence.

III.   Complete the crossword puzzle using the clues below.

Across

1. lightning never _____ in the same place

4. nothing hurts like _____

7. _____ travels fast

8. _____ is good news

10. the proof of the _____ is the eating

12. might makes _____

13. after the feast comes _____

Down

1. good things come in _____

2. it never rains but _____

3. _____ is nine-tenths of the law

5. the bigger they are, the _____

6. _____ in life are free

9. _____ is better than foresight

11. the grass is always _____ on the other side of the fence

Answer Key

I. 1. a.
    2. a.
    3. b.
    4. b.
    5. b.
    6. a.
    7. c.
    8. c.
    9. a.
    10. a.
    11. c.
    12. c.
    13. b.
    14. b.

II. 1. f.
    2. k.
    3. m.
    4. c.
    5. i.
    6. j.
    7. a.
    8. g.
    9. h.
    10. b.
    11. l.
    12. d.
    13. n.
    14. e.

III.

```
 1                          2          3
 S T R I K E S T W I C E    P
 M                    T      O      4   5                 6
 7                    T      S      T H E T R U T H
 B A D N E W S        P      S          A                 H
                      8             E   R                 H
                      N O N E W S   S   D                 E
           9          U              S  E                 B
          10 H        R              S  R                 E
 P U D D I N G        S                 E                 S
 A       N   R                          S                 T
 C       D   E                12         T                T
 K       S   E                R I G H T  H                H
 A       I   E                      O    E                I
 G       G   N                      N    Y                N
 E           E                           F                G
 13          E                           A                S
 S   T H E R E C K O N I N G              L
     T                                    L
```